CONTENTS

HEROES

INCREDIBLE TRUE STORIES OF COURAGEOUS ANIMALS

DAVID LONG

Illustrated by Kerry Hyndman

90 YEARS OF EXCELLENCE

FABER & FABER

For my Rosy, with love and gratitude

First published in the UK in 2014 under the title *Jet the Rescue Dog*
This illustrated edition first published in the UK in 2018
This illustrated edition first published in the USA in 2018
by Faber and Faber Limited
Bloomsbury House
74–77 Great Russell Street
London WC1B 3DA
This paperback edition first published in 2019

Designed by Faber and Faber
Printed in China

A CIP record for this book is available from the British Library

978-0-571-34629–5

2 4 6 8 10 9 7 5 3 1

For as long as there have been wars, animals have been out there saving lives. Over the years cats, dogs, horses and even birds have shown incredible courage and devotion, and this book tells some of their extraordinary stories.

Not all of these adventures have happy endings, but every one is true. They show us the unique bond that can develop between animal and man. By reminding us that not all heroes are human, they also cast a shining light on some of the worst moments in a hundred years of history.

Rip: a rescuer among the ruins
The Blitz, Second World War, London, 1940

When we watch the news after a natural disaster such as an earthquake or tornado we often see dogs on television helping police and soldiers look for people buried in the rubble. These animals are highly trained and form an important part of the teams which specialise in this kind of urban search and rescue. Amazingly, the first dog ever to do this had no training at all, and yet Rip was one of the best when it came to finding survivors.

1

During the Second World War, in 1940, the wire-haired terrier turned up at the scene of an air raid in East London. No one knew who he was or why he was there. I don't suppose he knew either, but when he saw people clambering over the ruins looking for survivors perhaps he thought it was a game and decided to join in.

No one knew who he was or why he was there

Terrible scenes of devastation were common during the Blitz, when more than a million homes, shops and factories were damaged or destroyed by enemy bombs falling on British cities. In London it was the job of Air Raid Precautions (ARP) wardens to warn people to take cover before each air raid. After the 'All Clear' was sounded these same ARP wardens led the search for survivors.

The terrier started following one of the wardens around, a man called Mr King. Mr King liked dogs and felt sorry for this particular one, which didn't have a collar and looked rather hungry. The dog seemed genuinely grateful when Mr King gave him a piece of sandwich left over from his supper, and soon joined Mr King when he went on his rounds each night, directing people to the safety of the air-raid shelters.

No collar meant no name tag, so Mr King decided to call his new friend Rip. He thought the little dog was probably homeless, as many were during the war. Thousands of families left London for the safety of the countryside, forgetting their cats and dogs in the rush to leave. Other pets lost their homes as a result of the air raids.

After one of these raids Mr King was searching the site of a burned-out factory. Rip saw what he was doing and started to sniff around. This is something dogs do instinctively as a way of understanding the world, and it is something they are incredibly good at.

Depending on its breed, a dog's nose is as much as ten million times more sensitive to smell than yours. A human nose has around five million scent-detecting cells but a dog has nearly three hundred million of them, and the reason a dog's nose is cold and wet is because this helps it capture even more scent.

A human nose has around five million scent-detecting cells but a dog has nearly three hundred million of them

Using just his nose, a dog like Rip is able to interpret the world in a way we could not hope to copy. When humans smell their lunch they just smell lunch, but a dog can detect every ingredient individually. Similarly, just as a particular scent might alert a person to the presence of another animal somewhere nearby, that same scent will tell a whole story to a dog: what kind of an animal it is, whether it is male or female, young or old, and even what mood it is likely to be in.

Knowing this, Mr King realised that Rip wasn't just sniffing around the ruined building for fun and that when he started wagging his tail it must be because he had found something interesting beneath the broken bricks and splintered timber.

The warden started digging and shortly afterwards, when a man was pulled alive from the rubble, Mr King realised that Rip had a real talent for finding people in trouble. It wasn't just Rip's superior sense of smell that helped him do this, but also his curiosity and inexhaustible energy. Best of all, because terriers are such small dogs, Rip was able to squeeze his way into spaces which were far too tight for a person to wriggle through.

The risks Rip faced while doing this were considerable. Often there were fires still burning inside the buildings, and occasionally unexploded bombs. The scale of destruction meant that walls could topple down at any time, and broken glass was a common problem. Rip refused to be scared by any of this, however, and his sense of adventure meant that as soon as a raid was over he was desperate to get stuck in. Clambering over the ruins, braving the smoke and flames, he went out night after night for as long as the raids continued.

Altogether Rip spent five years on duty, and he was soon famous in London for having what we call a sixth sense when it came to finding survivors. Sometimes the other wardens would want to call a halt and go home, convinced they had searched every square centimetre of a burned-out factory or warehouse. But Mr King knew that if Rip refused to leave the site it was because somehow he knew that someone was still trapped and needed their help.

If Rip refused to leave the site it was because somehow he knew that someone was still trapped and needed help

Rip simply never got it wrong. His super-sensitive nose, the sight of his short stubby tail wagging rapidly from side to side, and above all the scrabbling noise of his little paws pushing away at a pile of bricks and tiles, were all the proof Mr King needed to keep looking. When Rip refused to give up the wardens would go back and search the ruins again – and every time the dog would be proved right and another person would be rescued.

This astonishing success rate meant that Rip soon had new friends all over his part of the city. In those days it was a very poor area and food was strictly rationed; but many of the locals still insisted on giving Rip a little treat whenever he trotted around the corner. His biggest fans weren't just the dozens of survivors he helped to rescue either, but also the people he met out on his nightly patrols with Mr King.

For all of them it must have been a frightening time to be living in the capital, but somehow having Rip around made things more bearable. He was such a happy character and was always pleased to see a new face. People also thought that if Rip could cope with the war then so could they.

His cheerful character and tireless enthusiasm ensured that he has never been forgotten

Most of all people hoped the fighting would end and that life could go back to normal, but sadly for Rip it never did. Exhausted by all his hard work, and perhaps weakened by inhaling smoke and fumes from so many burning factories and other buildings, his little heart eventually gave up. When it did he was buried in a new cemetery created for animal heroes at Ilford in Essex, but his cheerful character and tireless enthusiasm ensured that he has never been forgotten. A few years ago a collector paid a fortune for the medal Rip used to wear on his collar, and today he is remembered as one of the pioneers who demonstrated how useful dogs can be when it comes to searching for survivors in peacetime as well as war.

GALLIPOLI MURPHY:
FOUR-LEGGED AMBULANCE
Battle of Gallipoli,
First World War, Turkey, 1915

Helicopters and specially equipped armoured vehicles are used to rescue troops injured in battle, but in the past soldiers who were wounded had to rely on other soldiers acting as stretcher-bearers to carry them to safety. Rescues likes this were difficult and dangerous, especially when heavy fighting meant stretcher-bearers could themselves be killed or injured. This is what happened in 1915 in a place called Gallipoli on the coast of Turkey, but luckily a plucky donkey called Murphy rode bravely to the rescue.

Thousands of soldiers from Australia and New Zealand had come under fire from Turkish army guns, and a stretcher-bearer called Private John Simpson soon found himself surrounded by men in urgent need of emergency medical treatment.

Carrying a man on a stretcher takes at least two people, and Private Simpson had no one around to help him. He had an idea, though, about how he might be able **Thousands of soldiers from Australia and New Zealand had come under fire** to rescue wounded soldiers without the help of anyone else. The previous day he had spotted a donkey grazing under some nearby trees. Armies used to use mules and donkeys to carry equipment and supplies on the battlefield, and Private Simpson was sure this one could help him move his injured comrades.

Very slowly he approached the donkey across the field, speaking softly so as not to scare it off. When he was close enough, he looped a rope around the donkey's neck as a sort of makeshift halter, and then led it back to where the men were lying. All the time he kept chatting in a quiet, reassuring manner, hoping to make friends with the donkey as well as keeping it from trying to run away from the guns.

Simpson decided to call his new companion Murphy, and over the next twenty-five days the two of them worked tirelessly bringing injured men to safety. Any who could walk were escorted to one of the first-aid posts which the Australian army had set up on the beach at Anzac Cove. The more badly wounded were carefully helped onto the donkey's back, and then slowly carried down to the shoreline.

With so many men killed and injured it was slow work. It was also extremely dangerous as the battle raged all around, the enemy firing on the fighting men as well as on Simpson and Murphy as they made their way down to the cove. Again and again they braved the gunfire, Murphy keeping his head down and his ears back, and Private Simpson trying to calm him by whistling and singing quietly by his side as the two of them walked on.

No one knows quite how many lives were saved by Private Simpson and Murphy

No one knows quite how many lives were saved by Private Simpson and Murphy in this way, but over the course of three weeks it must have been at least a hundred, maybe more. Tramping up and down to the cove night and day, and snatching only short rests every now and then, the pair were somehow able to ignore the danger and the terrifying noise all around them. No matter how fierce the fighting, if there was an injured man out on the battlefield who needed their help the pair would go and find him.

To those they rescued, Murphy must have seemed like a sort of lucky charm, but his example sent a positive message to the other soldiers, too. The sight of the courageous pair steadfastly plodding up and down to the beach put new heart into even the most exhausted of them, almost as if the donkey realised how important his work was as a kind of four-legged ambulance.

Because he saved so many lives, and encouraged the troops not to give up, 'Gallipoli Murphy' is now remembered as one of Australia's real wartime heroes. Depicted in paintings, photographs and even statues, as the country's most famous donkey he has even appeared on postage stamps and as the star of a movie called *Murphy of Anzac*.

JUDY: ANIMAL PRISONER OF WAR

From Singapore to Burma, Second World War, South-east Asia, 1942

When their gunboat HMS *Grasshopper* was refuelling in the Chinese city of Shanghai a group of Royal Navy sailors saw a brown and white puppy for sale. She was a lively pointer, a breed with a reputation for being fun and friendly, so they bought her, called her Judy and took her on board.

In 1942 the *Grasshopper* was docked at the British naval base at

Singapore when it came under attack from the Japanese. The crew managed to sail out of the harbour just in time, but were then spotted by the pilots of two enemy aircraft. Hit by several shells, the gunboat sank very quickly, but not before Judy and the sailors had leapt overboard and started swimming towards the nearest shore – a tiny, inhospitable Indonesian island.

Hit by several shells, the gunboat sank very quickly

Once on dry land the men thought they were safe, but very quickly their mood changed from relief to despair. They had escaped from Singapore, and had survived the sinking of the *Grasshopper*. But now they could find nothing to eat on the small island and, even more worryingly, no source of fresh water. Without water to drink the sailors knew they wouldn't last more than a few days, and without a boat none of them could imagine how they could get off the island.

They were still wondering what to do when one of the sailors noticed Judy down by the shore. Wet and bedraggled from the swim, she was pawing excitedly at a patch of ground. It looked as though she had found something interesting, and a couple of the men ran over to see what it was. Ignoring them Judy started digging furiously, and then stuck her head down into the hole and began drinking.

The two sailors were overjoyed: like humans, dogs don't drink seawater, so the men realised straight away that Judy must have found a freshwater spring. One of them knelt down to drink himself, and within moments all the sailors were jostling around Judy's new waterhole waiting for their turn to quench their thirst.

After refreshing themselves in this way the crew had a second stroke of luck when Judy started barking at a Chinese junk (a type of sailing boat) which her sharp eyes had spotted on the horizon. By waving and shouting the sailors managed to attract the captain's attention, and as the junk drew nearer to investigate a few of them swam out to meet it. When the captain heard their story he agreed to take everybody to the much larger island of Sumatra, which the men thought might be safer. Together with Judy, they all piled on board.

The journey to Sumatra was uneventful, but when they got there it must have felt as though their troubles were just beginning. Unfortunately, to reach the safest part of the island the group had a gruelling three hundred kilometre trek ahead of them, most of it through dense rainforest. Luckily they were all fit young men, but the going was tough and they knew there were enemy troops on the attack in some parts of the island.

Days were spent cutting a path through the jungle and each night they would have to find somewhere to rest until dawn. At first this arrangement worked well enough, but then one morning they awoke to find themselves surrounded by enemy soldiers. Exhausted and unarmed, the men realised they would have to surrender. They were forced to climb into the back of a lorry which had arrived to take them away, and with Judy hidden beneath a pile of empty rice sacks, they were driven off to a prisoner of war camp.

Exhausted and unarmed, the men realised they would have to surrender

The camp was many kilometres away, and everyone was parched and hungry by the time they got there, including Judy. It soon became apparent that prison rations were barely enough to survive on, but that didn't stop

Frank Williams, a twenty-three-year-old airman in the camp, offering the dog some of his food. It was only a tiny portion of maggoty rice but this small gesture was the beginning of an important friendship for both of them, a friendship which would see Frank and Judy through many years of hardship and suffering at the hands of the prison guards.

In tough times, good friends are important. Forced to endure terrible living conditions and regular beatings, Frank looked upon Judy as the best friend he could possibly have. It wasn't just that he found her such good company. He also admired her uncanny instinct for danger (she always barked if there was a snake or poisonous scorpion anywhere near) and he was sure that, as one of nature's survivors, Judy was a lucky charm.

Many of the sailors from the *Grasshopper* felt much the same way, convinced that if a dog could survive the harsh jungle conditions then they certainly could. Her habit of barking loudly whenever one of the guards appeared cheered them up a lot too, but of course this made Judy very unpopular with the camp authorities.

She became the world's first ever animal prisoner of war

The prisoners loved watching Judy giving the guards a hard time, but after a few weeks one guard in particular had had enough and threatened to shoot her if she didn't stop hassling him in this way. Frank was horrified by this; Judy was his best friend after all, and he asked the camp commandant to do something to protect her. The commandant agreed to make Judy's status official, which he thought might stop the guards shooting her. As 'Prisoner No. 81A' she became the world's first ever animal prisoner of war.

No one was ever quite sure why the commandant was happy to help in this way but perhaps he was worried that if the dog was harmed by one of the guards the men might protest by causing a riot. It is also possible that he had heard a rumour that Judy was expecting puppies, and that as an animal lover he was hoping to get a puppy in exchange for protecting her.

The rumour turned out to be true, and a few weeks later Judy gave birth to nine puppies. (The prisoners assumed that the father was a guard dog, although they were never sure.) One of the puppies was handed over to the commandant, and for a while life became more bearable for Frank and his comrades.

Their relief was to be short-lived, however. A few weeks later the prisoners were told that they were to be moved to a different camp. To get to this new camp the men had to board another ship, and naturally Frank was determined to find a way to take Judy with him. The only thing he could think of was to put her into another rice sack over his shoulder so he could smuggle her on board. He knew she would have to be in the sack for several hours. He wondered if he could carry her for that long (pointers are quite big dogs) and if Judy would be able to stay still and quiet.

Judy managed to stay completely still and silent for more than three hours

Amazingly, she could! Despite the sweaty heat of the jungle and the discomfort of lying upside down in the dark, Judy managed to stay completely still and silent for more than three hours. Frank was so proud of her, and very relieved when they got on the ship and he could put her down. Frank had no idea at this stage where they were going to, but as soon as they set sail he started looking for a secret hiding place. After a few minutes he found somewhere down below deck where Judy would stay safe and hidden.

If anything the ship turned out to be even more uncomfortable than the camp. There were no threats from the guards, but with more than seven hundred prisoners squeezed into every nook and cranny, conditions below deck were suffocating. No one had enough room to lie down properly or to move around, and the only food and water were what the prisoners had managed to steal from the camp.

It must have seemed like things couldn't get any worse, but then above the throbbing din of the ship's engines came the unmistakeable sound of aircraft, followed by loud gunfire. The men realised they were under attack, presumably by a British pilot who didn't realise that the ship was carrying prisoners of war.

The attack didn't last long, because in no time at all a torpedo dropped from the aeroplane found its mark, blowing a huge hole in the side of the ship. The men felt it lurch to one side and then, as water rushed into the hole, the ship began to sink, fast, very fast.

The men in Frank Williams' section were trapped by a locked door, but he tried desperately to save Judy's life by lifting her up and squeezing her through a broken porthole. Frank knew she could swim, as she had managed to reach that first tiny island. Now his only hope was that they were near enough land for her to take her chance and swim to safety.

Judy disappeared into the sea with a loud splash. For the first time since the two of them had got together in the prison camp, Frank Williams felt scared and lonely. With his friend gone and night falling fast, he knew there was nothing more he could do. He was trapped in a sinking ship, thousands

He was trapped in a sinking ship, thousands of kilometres from home

of kilometres from home, and it looked as though everyone in his section of the ship was going to drown.

Frank and his comrades must have felt that all was lost, but then something extraordinary happened. When the torpedo had hit the ship there had been a tremendous explosion and now, suddenly, there was another one which was even louder. The noise was terrifying, and the ship took another big lurch as if it was going to turn right over.

As the smoke cleared, however, Frank Williams realised something remarkable: he could see the sky. The second explosion had ripped through the ship's hull, leaving a long jagged hole down one side. This meant the ship would sink even more quickly, but it also provided a possible way out for the men.

Frank was one of the first men to clamber through the opening, and he and several others dropped down into the cold water. They were unable to see much in the dark, and Frank had no idea how close they were to land. But, like Judy, he could at least take his chances now rather than being trapped in the stricken vessel. As for Judy, she was nowhere to be seen, but Frank hoped that she had somehow been able to swim to safety.

They were safe, but bound for a new prison camp – and, sadly, there was no sign of Judy

After several hours drifting around in the water he and the other men were picked up by another Japanese boat which was heading for Singapore. They were safe, but bound for a new prison camp – and, sadly, there was no sign of Judy. One sailor thought he had seen a dog paddling around in the water before the ship sank. Another said she had been holding a piece of broken plank in her jaws so that survivors would have something to hold

on to. No one was able to say what had happened to her after that, however, and Frank sadly concluded she had probably drowned.

*

It took the men three days to reach the new prison camp, by which time they were hungry and exhausted. Most of them just wanted to lie down and

Judy must somehow have managed to swim ashore

rest, but as they were pushed and shoved through the heavily armed gate by the guards something truly wonderful happened. 'I couldn't believe my eyes,' Williams later told a newspaper reporter. 'As I entered the camp, a scraggy dog hit me square between the shoulders and knocked me over! I'd never been so glad to see the old girl, and I think she felt the same.' Judy must somehow have managed to swim ashore!

Although it was the happiest of reunions, the two friends were still far from safe. Frank and the other prisoners were now forced to spend more than a year labouring in the jungle for their captors. Working punishingly long hours, with only rotting food to eat and filthy river water to drink, they suffered regular beatings from the brutal guards and were frequently sick.

The men were building what became known as the 'Death Railway'. It was called this because before the war ended more than a hundred thousand prisoners and Asian slave labourers had died laying tracks for more than four hundred kilometres from Burma to Thailand. Frank was one of the survivors, though, and he later said it was all thanks to Judy, who gave him a reason to live. 'All I had to do was look at her and into those weary, bloodshot eyes and I would ask myself: What would happen to her if I died?'

Fortunately, despite the cruelty and the hardship they endured, there were some happy moments too. After the war Williams told many stories of Judy in the prison camp – of her chasing monkeys through the trees, barking at flying foxes, spending hours trying to bury a huge elephant bone, and spooking the guards by running after them with an old skull clamped in her jaws. Most of all though they were tales of two old pals, who did everything they could to see each other through hard times.

Despite all this, and Judy's popularity and unswerving loyalty to the men, the army refused to consider bringing her back to England when the war finally ended. Frank and his friends had a plan, however, and once again their special dog was bundled into a sack and smuggled on board the ship carrying them back to Liverpool.

Weeks later, when they docked in England, Judy got the welcome she deserved. She was invited to London to be made an official member of the Returned British Prisoners of War Association, the only dog ever to be honoured in this way.

An official member of the Returned British Prisoners of War Association, the only dog ever to be honoured in this way

She got a medal, and so did Frank Williams, recognising the devotion he had shown to Judy and his ingenuity in bringing her safely back home.

The two friends then spent a year travelling around the country visiting the relatives of those who had died working on the terrible Death Railway. Judy was always a great comfort to the families she and Frank Williams met, just as she had been for the prisoners in the camps.

PETER: THE DOG WHO WAS KISSED BY A QUEEN

The Blitz, Second World War, London, 1944

Some dogs can seem impossible to train, and Peter the Scotch collie appeared to be one of the worst. When his family in Birmingham took him out he would constantly pull at the lead and attack any other dogs he saw. And if they left him at home they would get back to find he had chewed all the furniture as well as any shoes which had been left lying around.

The family was reluctant to get rid of him as Peter was a handsome dog who had cost them quite a lot to buy as a puppy. But furniture and footwear were expensive too, and by June 1944 the Stables family had had enough and decided to give him away. The army seemed like the best place, although Mrs Stables thought she ought to warn them that in her opinion the destructive dog was something of a four-legged gangster.

In her opinion the destructive dog was something of a four-legged gangster

Army dogs had to be brave, disciplined and patient, none of which sounded like Peter. The army took him on anyway, perhaps thinking that some of the worst pets made the best workers. Sometimes this can happen, and with only a few weeks' training this previously unruly animal began to show a real talent for learning new skills.

In particular, Peter demonstrated to his trainers that he was extremely good at following instructions. Never panicking at the sound of gunfire, and clearly exceptionally intelligent, Peter's performance in test after test was so good that his trainer began to wonder whether his previous bad behaviour had just been his way of showing that he was bored and needed a challenge.

If so, Peter was about to discover that war wasn't boring, and that the army could certainly find him a new challenge. At the height of the German V1 and V2 rocket attacks which were causing yet more deaths and destruction in London in 1944, Peter was loaded into an army truck, driven up to London and put to work searching for victims and survivors of the terrible raids.

By this time there were several other dogs in the capital doing similar work, but few, if any of them, were as good as Peter. Fast and accurate, and with a very good sense of smell, he was able to pinpoint exactly where a survivor was so that rescuers didn't waste time digging in the wrong area. Each time he found someone he quickly moved on to the next search, never wasting time or getting in the way of the rescue squads.

He was able to pinpoint exactly where a survivor was so that rescuers didn't waste time digging in the wrong area

Rarely showing any signs of getting tired, Peter would often keep working for twelve hours without a rest. He also had a remarkable ability to concentrate for extended periods of time, and would be hard at it long after his human handlers had become exhausted. Admittedly he once found a parrot when everyone else expected to find a person, but then, to be fair to Peter, it was a talking parrot so he could be forgiven for getting confused!

Aside from this there was only one occasion when Peter disappointed the people he worked alongside. For no apparent reason he and another search dog suddenly started misbehaving and refused to search the areas they were told to. It must have looked as though he was returning to his bad old ways, but actually he was protesting because no one had fed him properly for two or three days. Food was often in very short supply during the war years, and the dogs were fed biscuits and water when what they really needed was meat.

Luckily some meat was found and put in their bowls, and as soon as he'd finished eating Peter was back to his usual fast and efficient self. Locating no fewer than three different survivors in three different places, and then a missing child, the star dog lost no time in showing that he was back on duty. After that he never let his performance slip again, as long as no one forgot to feed him.

When the war ended in 1945 Peter was chosen to lead a celebration parade through Hyde Park in London. It was a great honour for him and his owners, particularly when they were presented to King George VI and his wife. The following day one of the newspapers reported that the Queen had kissed Peter on the nose. Today he is remembered as the bad dog who, with a little help and understanding, became very good indeed.

GUSTAV: THE FIRST BIRD BACK FROM THE BATTLE

The D-Day Landings, Second World War, northern France, 1944

Special pigeons travelled on aeroplanes, and others were parachuted into enemy territory with secret agents or went into battle with journalists whose job it was to report on how the war was going.

The pigeons were vital because in wartime it isn't always possible to report the news by telephone. Also military secrecy meant reporters had to maintain 'radio silence' so that pigeons like Gustav often provided the only way to get an all-important report back from the front line.

In the whole of the Second World War, D-Day was one of the most important military operations, a huge naval, army and air force campaign to cross the English Channel and recapture France from the Germans. Involving the largest invasion force ever assembled – hundreds of thousands of British, American and Canadian troops, and thousands of ships and aircraft – it had to be conducted in conditions of absolute secrecy.

D-Day was one of the most important military operations

If it was successful it could help end the war at last, so none of the reporters wanted to miss it. Because it was so hazardous only a few of them were given permission to travel with the troops. The pigeons were provided so that they could send brief reports back to their newspapers in London, describing what they could see and how the battle was progressing.

Gustav was one of those birds, and he travelled with a war correspondent called Montague Taylor. Taylor had four birds with him because he knew the battle to liberate France would be a long one. Gustav was the best of them, however, and had already completed several missions carrying top secret information back from agents in Belgium.

This time he was released from a battleship carrying troops to France. His message read: *We are just twenty miles or so off the beaches. First assault troops landed 0750. Signal says no interference from enemy gunfire on beach. Passage uneventful. Steaming steadily in formation. Lightnings, Typhoons, Fortresses [aircraft] crossing since 0545. No enemy aircraft seen.*

It is a very short note but historically a very significant one. Gustav had delivered the first report to reach England on what turned out to be a critically important day for everyone involved in the European war. Thousands of men died, and tens of thousands were injured, but the invasion was successful and led to the eventual downfall, after more than five years, of the enemy.

Gustav had delivered the first report to reach England on what turned out to be a critically important day

France and England are separated by not much more than thirty kilometres of water, but to reach his home loft Gustav had to fly in a huge circuit which took him nearly two hundred and fifty kilometres. This meant braving the battle that was raging all around him, and flying through gunfire, mortar explosions and thick smoke from all the warships and aircraft supporting the invasion.

A second pigeon was sent back with a message describing exactly what this was like: *Shells exploding all over beach and out at sea as wave after wave of Allied ships as far as eye can see sweeping into shore.* And a third carried a message from a reporter describing what he could see from his dugout: *bombs, shells, bullets and mines, to say nothing of booby traps, which make each hour an age of grim experience.*

Of course these were the lucky ones because, inevitably, many other birds did not make it home at all. Even Gustav, fit and fast as he was, took five hours and sixteen minutes to reach his loft in Hampshire. But, braving bullets and overcoming an animal's natural fear of smoke and gunfire, he flew through the chaos of the battle to bring home the best possible news: that the war, finally, was beginning to come to an end.

ROB: THE DOG WHO JOINED THE SAS
The Battle of Tunisia, Second World War, North Africa, 1943

Rob the collie was one of the army's first paradogs and he made more than twenty parachute jumps during his time with the Special Forces. Most famously, he was dropped deep into enemy territory when British, American and Canadian paratroopers were fighting hard to regain control of Italy and North Africa.

It must have been an extraordinary adventure for the dog who grew up on a cattle farm in rural Shropshire. Mostly black, with white legs and a distinctive patch on his face, Rob was about four years old when his family decided to volunteer him for war work.

Most dogs of this sort were set to work guarding military bases in Britain, but soon after joining the army Rob was shipped out to North Africa to guard prisoners of war in a desert camp.

Fortunately Rob didn't mind the ferocious heat. Clearly a bright dog, he learned how to perform new tasks very quickly. Because he seemed unusually intelligent, a soldier called Quartermaster Major Burt began to wonder if he wasn't wasted doing simple guard duties. Like the men in the Special Air Service, thought Burt, Rob appeared to have special talents. He seemed like the sort of resourceful animal who could put stealth, silence and strength to good purpose, working with those soldiers who were sent into the enemy's territory to blow up military facilities and disrupt their plans.

Fitted the dog with a borrowed parachute harness so the two of them could jump out of the plane

To test this theory QM Burt is thought to have smuggled Rob onto an aeroplane one night to see how he reacted to the noise and motion of flying. Rob turned out to be quite happy with this, so QM Burt tried again and on a second flight fitted the dog with a borrowed parachute harness so the two of them could jump out of the plane!

Once again Rob appeared to be completely unfazed by the experience, and actually seemed to enjoy it. Convinced he was on to something, his new master asked his commanding officer for permission to carry on with the training. Over the next few weeks Rob completed more than a dozen practice jumps, and on several occasions appeared to be so enthusiastic that he had to be prevented from being the first one to jump out of the plane.

Back in Shropshire the family received a note from the army telling them Rob was fit and well, and doing 'a splendid job of work'. Because he was with the Special Air Service, which often carries out top secret work in dangerous areas, the note said nothing about where he was or what he was actually doing. In fact by this time Rob is thought to have been rounding up enemy parachutists who had been sent to reinforce German and Italian troops in Tunisia. As humans their night vision was nowhere near as good as a dog's; by helping to capture them Rob assisted in the Allied invasion of that country, which eventually led to the enemy's surrender.

During this period Rob made at least two more parachute jumps himself, possibly three, on each occasion risking his life to help the men he served alongside. This wasn't just due to the obvious risks of bailing out of an aircraft. Infuriated by British successes in the desert war, the Nazi leader Adolf Hitler had also ordered that from now on parachutists were to be shot on sight rather than taken prisoner.

Because the SAS doesn't discuss its missions there are still plenty of secrets surrounding Rob's time with them. It is known that one of his jumps was part of an operation to rescue some airmen and soldiers who had been taken prisoner in Italy. There are also official government documents confirming that Rob's presence on raiding parties behind enemy lines 'saved many of them from being discovered,

> Rob saved many of them from being discovered, and thereby from being captured and killed

and thereby from being captured and killed'. In this his keen eyesight and hearing would have been invaluable because a good dog will often detect something or find someone a human would miss.

Rob eventually received no fewer than seven medals and awards, but even now much of his time with the army remains shrouded in mystery. When the war finally ended in 1945 he was returned to his family in Shropshire, and after so long they were very happy to have him back. Unfortunately Rob's training meant that for a while he was better at rounding the children up than the farm animals, but gradually he learned to relax and was soon back to being an ordinary family pet.

VOYTEK: THE BEAR WHO CARRIED BOMBS

The Battle of Monte Cassino, Second World War, from Iran to Italy, then Edinburgh, 1944

Poland was the first country to be invaded at the start of the Second World War, but many soldiers and airmen escaped from the country and were able to fight on the side of the Allies. More than a hundred thousand of them joined the Polish II Army Corps, and together with a mountain bear called

Voytek they fought alongside British and Commonwealth troops in the Middle East and North Africa before taking part in one of the most ferocious battles of the whole war.

In 1942 some of these soldiers had found themselves stationed in the ancient city of Hamadan in Iran. Sent there to capture some strategically important oilfields, they had been approached by a young boy who had found a bear cub living alone in the woods. Thinking its mother had probably been killed by hunters, the boy said the cub was an orphan. It was too small to survive on its own, but the boy couldn't have it at home and hoped the soldiers might keep it as their mascot.

The soldiers liked this idea and agreed to buy the bear in exchange for a couple of tins of meat for the boy and his family. Thinking it would be fun to have him around, they called him Voytek, a Polish word meaning 'Smiling Warrior'.

Despite his name, Voytek was anything but a warrior. He was much too friendly for that, and so small that for a while he used to sleep in a washing-up bowl. Because he was still only a baby the soldiers had difficulty getting him to eat anything, but with a bit of help he learned to drink milk from an old vodka bottle. As the weeks turned into months he gradually moved on to eating figs and dates, as well as honey (like Winnie the Pooh) and even jars of marmalade (like Paddington Bear).

Despite his name, Voytek was anything but a warrior

During his time with the soldiers he picked up a few bad habits as well. Watching them marching around the camp, Voytek learned to salute, but he also started smoking cigarettes and drinking beer, which became his absolutely favourite thing, although it would not have been good for his health. If he had too much to drink he would then break into the stores and steal more food, and more than once he pulled a lot of underwear off a washing line, and was caught parading around with it all wrapped around his head. He would also sneak into the showers to fool around, and after learning how to use the taps he managed to waste all the water before anyone realised what was going on.

As he grew larger and stronger Voytek also liked to wrestle with the men, but never fiercely, as he just wanted to be friends with everyone. Even in later life, by which time he was almost two metres tall and had a formidable set of fifteen-centimetre claws, there was never any sign of him becoming savage, which many wild animals will do as they reach maturity.

As the war progressed, the Poles travelled hundreds of kilometres west to Egypt. In 1944 their orders were to cross the Mediterranean and join thousands of other troops fighting the German army in Italy. Naturally they wanted Voytek to go with them, but no one would let them bring a bear on board ship. The men were desperate, and, sensing their unhappiness, Voytek was also becoming upset. In order to make it possible for him to travel a helpful **No one would let** senior officer decided to enlist him into the **them bring a bear on** Polish army as a private. Once this was done **board ship** and he had the correct paperwork showing his name, rank and number, it was agreed that he could travel into battle.

Until now Voytek had been a lot of fun for the men, but in Italy the men needed his help as well as his company. Soon after arriving they found

themselves fighting in the Battle of Monte Cassino, one of the most bitter and destructive campaigns in the whole of the war.

Thousands of British, American, French and Commonwealth troops were brought in to dislodge a well-armed enemy from a fortress-like abbey positioned high on a rocky hill. More than one thousand two hundred and fifty tons of bombs were dropped onto the hill over a period of a day and a night, and the thousand-year-old abbey was left in ruins, but there was no surrender. It was decided to launch a huge artillery barrage, and the Polish soldiers were given the responsibility for keeping an estimated two thousand big guns supplied with ammunition.

The enemy continued to return fire, making the work hard and exceptionally dangerous, but even with their own lives in danger the soldiers were concerned about Voytek. They could see that such a large animal presented an easy, obvious target to an enemy sniper and tried to get him under cover. But Voytek refused to hide, even though to begin with he was clearly scared by the noise of so many explosions.

Voytek refused to hide, even though to begin with he was clearly scared by the noise of so many explosions

He quickly became braver, however, and as the fighting continued there were numerous eye-witness accounts of him actually helping his comrades. Far from cowering in fear, Voytek was seen carrying one giant shell after another from the Polish supply depot forward to the Allies' guns.

Unsurprisingly this caused some concern, and not just because bears aren't often seen in Italy. The biggest worry was that a great clumsy bear might drop one of the shells, with potentially disastrous results, but the soldiers who knew Voytek best insisted he could be trusted. No one knows precisely how many shells he carried, but during the course of the battle the Polish II Corps delivered an incredible seventeen thousand tons of ammunition to the front-line troops and more than one thousand tons of food.

This was obviously a major contribution to the Allies' eventual victory, and Voytek's part in it has never been forgotten. From then until the end of the war Polish artillery supply vehicles were painted with a picture of a bear carrying a shell, and the legend of the 'soldier bear' became an inspirational symbol of freedom for Poles everywhere who were fighting to regain their country.

The legend of the 'soldier bear' became an inspirational symbol of freedom

In the end they were successful, and a year after the victory at Monte Cassino, Poland was back in Polish hands and the soldiers could return home. None of them could really afford to keep a bear so Voytek was given to Edinburgh Zoo, where he lived happily for the next twenty years. He still enjoyed the odd cigarette thrown into his enclosure by Polish visitors who knew his story, but with no one to light them he used to eat them instead.

After his death, statues of Voytek were erected in London and in Krakow in Poland, and a third was unveiled in Edinburgh to mark the seventieth anniversary of the Battle of Monte Cassino – Voytek's battle.

SATAN OF VERDUN:
A CITY'S SAVIOUR

The Siege of Verdun, First World War, northern France, 1916

In 1916 the city of Verdun in France was the setting for one of the longest and most ferocious battles of the First World War. Tens of thousands of French troops took part in the fighting, but in the end it was left to a huge black dog called Satan to play a crucial role in its defence.

German forces attempted to capture the city, and more than eight hundred thousand men were killed or injured. Towards the end a group of French soldiers found themselves cut off from the main army and coming under heavy fire. When the last of their ammunition ran out the defenders had no way of saving themselves or their city, and without food or water surrender seemed to be their only option.

If they did this the soldiers knew Verdun would be destroyed, for the enemy's biggest guns had been shelling the walls for days. Worse still, if the French lost a historic fortress town like Verdun the loss of morale could mean they would lose the war as well. Because of this it was vital to get reinforcements through together with new supplies of guns and ammunition.

In situations like this, specially trained dogs and pigeons were often used to carry messages from the trenches back to headquarters. (The army had used telegraph cables to do this at first, but these were quickly destroyed by shelling.) The animals could run much faster than even an Olympic sprinter, and they were less likely to be shot than a soldier because they were much smaller. Pigeons could travel one hundred and fifty kilometres or more, but carried only very short messages rolled up in a tiny canister attached to one leg. Using larger circular containers strapped to a dog's back meant letters could be sent, or even a small amount of ammunition, but only over a distance of a few kilometres.

Unfortunately the French had no pigeons left, and their last dog had been sent back to headquarters with an important message several days earlier. Cold, wet, scared and very hungry, all the soldiers could do now was hunker down in one of the trenches and try to think of a way out of their terrible predicament.

While they were deciding what to do, one soldier looked over the top of the trench and through the smoke of the enemy's guns saw what appeared to be a miraculous vision. Racing towards him at top speed was an immense black beast, its jaws wide open and its eyes blazing. As it made its way across the battlefield, all four paws pounding the earth, the soldier could see what looked like great wings on either side of its body.

Racing towards him at top speed was an immense black beast, its jaws wide open and its eyes blazing

Unsurprisingly the soldier thought he was imagining things, for this didn't look like any animal he had ever seen before. The dark shape got closer and closer until eventually he recognised it as one of the garrison's messenger dogs. It was a lurcher called Satan, a crossbreed whose father had been a racing greyhound, making him one of the fastest runners in the whole of the French army.

The soldier realised the dog must have covered five kilometres at least, and he was astounded by his speed. It's not hard to imagine how excited (and how relieved) his comrades must have been too, when he shouted along the trench telling them to come and see what was happening. Peering carefully over the top of the trench a few of them began to cheer Satan on, but then suddenly they heard the loud crack of a sniper's rifle.

To their horror, the huge dog staggered to one side as a bullet tore into his side. The men ducked back into the safety of the trench. When it seemed safe to look up again Satan was back on his feet, but he was much slower now. Then another shot rang out and he collapsed back into the mud with a badly wounded leg.

The men realised their last hope was gone, disappearing as quickly as Satan had appeared out of nowhere just moments earlier. But then, to their amazement and delight, the brave dog once more hauled himself back up to his feet. Reeling and dizzy, and moving as fast as he could manage on three legs, he painfully limped the last few dozen metres before tumbling down into the trench.

> The brave dog once more hauled himself back up to his feet

When the soldiers saw the dog up close, it became clear what the first soldier had seen: Satan's 'wings' were actually two special baskets, each containing a carrier pigeon trained to fly back to the army's headquarters as quickly as possible. Using the birds the soldiers were able send a message describing where they were trapped and where the enemy guns were positioned. Sadly, the first bird they released never made it back to HQ, but the second delivered the hastily scrawled message within just minutes, and very soon the enemy guns were put out of action.

The men were saved, the city of Verdun was saved – and all thanks to a fast and fearless dog called Satan.

RATS: THE ARMY'S LITTLE DOG SOLDIER
Northern Ireland, 1976

In the second half of the twentieth century, thousands of British troops were permanently stationed in Northern Ireland. Over a period of more than thirty years what became known as the Troubles claimed more than three thousand six hundred lives. Many more – both soldiers and civilians – were injured during vicious campaigns of bombing and intimidation by rival groups of terrorists.

Not everyone welcomed the sight of armed troops on their streets, but one small brown and white terrier was always pleased to see a man in uniform. After encountering his first group of soldiers in the small town of Crossmaglen he began to hang around the barracks. When the men went out on patrol he would always trot along beside them, and then follow them back when they returned to camp.

Not everyone welcomed the sight of armed troops on their streets

With no sign of an owner, the soldiers decided to keep him. They called him Rats, and the little terrier was soon a familiar face around the town. Rats had a cheerful character, and found lots of ways of keeping the soldiers entertained when they were off-duty. For example, one of the soldiers had a mouth organ, and whenever he played a tune on it Rats would always sing along. The effect wasn't particularly musical, but the tuneless howls and growls made the men laugh and took their minds off the dangerous work they had to do.

Rats liked to pull and chew the men's bootlaces too, something which might have been annoying had they not enjoyed the dog's company so much. Having Rats around, one of them said, was a bit like having a mischievous child in the camp – and, like a child, he was fun and often made them laugh.

Out on patrol Rats was in as much danger as the men, particularly when the terrorists found out what he was up to. They knew Rats was good for the soldiers' morale and the fact that he cheered them up was enough to make him a target. On several occasions attempts were made to kill Rats, and during his time in Northern Ireland he was blown up, run over and shot at several times. But he was one of life's survivors, and the troops refused to leave him behind. Despite a broken leg, minor gunshot wounds and some pieces of bomb fragment (called shrapnel) lodged in his back, Rats rarely missed a patrol.

For the soldiers he was a good companion, but his natural instinct for danger was also something they could rely on. Several soldiers were convinced that Rats's alertness and vigilance was helping keep them and their comrades safe, so even on longer patrols they would insist on taking him up in the helicopters they used to move about the country.

Rats's alertness and vigilance was helping keep them and their comrades safe

When the media heard about Rats several reporters and even a BBC film crew were sent from London to investigate. By this time he was patrolling Crossmaglen and the surrounding area regularly, and his first television appearance turned him into a bit of star. Soon, so many people in England were sending cards and messages to Rats that the army had to open a special department to deal with his fan mail.

Rats was devoted to the soldiers, just as they were to him. But his story has a sad side to it as well. Individual regiments would do what's called a 'tour of duty', after which the soldiers were sent back to England. Poor little Rats wasn't allowed to go with them and so each time he made friends with a group of soldiers he would then be left behind while they returned home.

Because he was such a friendly dog it wouldn't take long for him to make new friends each time the new group of soldiers arrived. This would lift his spirits, and theirs too of course, and in no time at all Rats would be back on patrol with a different group of men. But it must have been very difficult for him even so, like a favourite pet who spends all his time with a family and then wakes up one morning to find them gone.

Eventually he did make it to England, but only after nearly three years of trying. In 1979 Rats was voted 'Dog of the Year' in a national competition. By this time he had been granted an official army number and, accompanied by two soldiers, the little hero was flown from Belfast to London to be presented with a special gold medal.

The medal had an image of the Queen on one side, and on the other his name and new army number 'Delta 777'. It also came with a certificate describing his 'Valour and Devotion to Duty, and for the comfort provided to soldiers serving in Crossmaglen'. When this was reported on television, and Rats was shown barking excitedly as everyone at the ceremony cheered, the amount of fan mail he was sent rocketed. At one point staff at the barracks were opening nearly three hundred letters and presents a day!

> **At one point the barracks were receiving nearly three hundred letters and presents a day**

Immediately after the ceremony Rats was flown back to Northern Ireland to continue his tour of duty, but by this time he was beginning to get old. After a period of illness (possibly caused by a rat bite) it was decided that Rats should retire, but for a while no one could decide what to do with him.

He couldn't stay in the barracks, but as a stray he had nowhere else to go. Many of the soldiers were also worried about his safety if he stayed in Crossmaglen, concerned that someone might attack Rats again in order to damage army morale. Because of this it was decided to take Rats back to England and to find him a new home in a secret location somewhere safe.

Plans were made to give him a new name, and after being banned from making any more television appearances Rats quietly disappeared from public life. Naturally the soldiers who served with Rats would miss seeing him around, but hopefully it was enough to know that their little dog soldier was away from danger and enjoying the happy retirement he so much deserved.

TOMMY: THE ACCIDENTAL SPY
Working for the Dutch Resistance, Second World War, Netherlands, 1942

Tommy was never meant to be a military pigeon, but became one after being blown off course during a race in 1942.

Tommy's owner had entered him for a race in Lancashire, and when the bird didn't return the owner probably assumed he was lost for good. In fact, Tommy had been blown across the North Sea, coming to rest in

the Netherlands, which by this time had been occupied by its enemies for nearly two years.

New laws meant that keeping pigeons was illegal, and the authorities were killing all the racing pigeons to prevent anyone using them to carry secret messages out of the country. Luckily, the person who found Tommy, a postman, had friends in the Dutch Resistance, a group of brave civilians working under cover to make life as hard as possible for the troops who had invaded their country. The work was highly skilled and very dangerous, and all of them knew that if they were caught using pigeons to send messages they would be tortured and imprisoned, or even killed.

The work was highly skilled and very dangerous

Tommy was handed over to one of the resistance fighters, a young man called Dick Drijver. Dick already had some experience of working with carrier pigeons, and despite the new laws he had hidden away a couple of his own birds, called Tijger and Amsterdammer. Guessing that Tommy was a British bird, he realised he might have found a way to get a message to the military in London.

Dick didn't know precisely where Tommy had come from, or who owned him, but this didn't matter. If he had come from England he would fly back to England once he had regained his strength. All Dick had to do was to hope that Tommy completed the journey and that his owner would know what to do with the message.

The message he planned to send concerned the location of a factory near Amsterdam where weapons were being manufactured. The Resistance wanted Britain's Royal Air Force to bomb it, thereby weakening the enemy's hold over the Dutch people. As soon as Tommy was fit enough to fly again the message was inserted into a tiny canister fixed to his leg, and with six hundred and fifty kilometres ahead of him he was launched on a journey back to the north of England.

A pigeon only weighs a few hundred grams, but they can fly so fast and for so long that Tommy reached home the following day. His owner, William Brockbank, couldn't believe it. Tommy had been missing for weeks, and now all of a sudden here he was back in his loft.

Mr Brockbank was also surprised to see his bird had a little canister on his leg with a note inside it. He couldn't understand the message (which was in code) but guessed it must be important and something to do with the war. It was passed on to the police immediately, and a few hours later it was decoded and handed over to the Royal Air Force.

At the time, everyone involved was sworn to secrecy, because if the story got out it would endanger the lives of Dick and his friends in the Dutch Resistance. After the war Tommy **After the war Tommy was declared a hero** was declared a hero, however, and in February 1946 Dick Drijver travelled to London to be reunited with his feathered friend. The two were presented with a medal by the head of the Dutch secret service, and to his great delight Dick received a gift of a pair of English pigeons to keep alongside Tijger and Amsterdammer.

RICKY: THE NOSE THAT KNEW
Minefield clearance, Second World War, Netherlands, 1944

As we have seen already, having a good sense of smell is an important life skill for a dog, and it is one we have often harnessed for our own purposes. For centuries dogs have been used to track wild animals for food as well as for locating people who are lost or enemies in hiding. For this sort of thing there is nothing better than a dog's nose, and even now, with all the advanced technology at its disposal, the army still relies on highly trained Arms and Explosives Search dogs.

With the right kind of training these dogs can check a suspicious vehicle for guns or other dangerous items far more quickly and more thoroughly than a human can. For example, searching the ground for mines and improvised explosive devices (or IEDs), a soldier with a metal detector might spend all day scanning an area the size of a football pitch. A dog can do the same thing in about an hour.

Other animals have been used too, including giant pouched rats from Africa, ordinary farm pigs and even honey bees – but dogs are the best. First used to search minefields during the Second World War, they have shown themselves to be fast and dependable, as well as making great companions for the men and women engaged in this painstaking and dangerous work.

In 1943 a new and particularly deadly type of mine was invented to kill anyone who stepped on it or wreck any vehicle driving over it. It was encased in wood or plastic instead of metal, which meant that an ordinary metal detector wouldn't work. Fortunately, dogs like Ricky could be trained to sniff out the explosive inside the mine, and very soon they were being used by British troops to make large areas of the battlefield safer.

Dogs like Ricky could be trained to sniff out the explosive inside the mine

Not every dog is suited to this sort of work, many of them being too excitable or unable to concentrate for the long periods required to get the job done. But others enjoy the work, and as well as being very good at it some have shown themselves to be exceptionally brave. Ricky was one of these, a Welsh collie sheepdog who refused to give up.

Ricky had been bought as a sixteen-week-old puppy by a lady from Kent called Mrs Litchfield. She offered him to the army, but only on condition that she got him back at the end of the war. The army agreed to this and in 1944 the dog was sent to the Netherlands with about sixty others. Over the winter he spent several months helping to clear mines from hundreds of kilometres of railway tracks and canal paths across the country.

The work was hard as well as dangerous. Thick snow and frozen ground made detection even trickier than usual, and a dozen different types of mine (some buried thirty centimetres underground) meant the dogs were often confused about what they were looking for. They mostly seemed to enjoy the hunt, however, and soldiers who saw Ricky at work said it cheered them up to see him excitedly criss-crossing the ground. Energetic, ears cocked and tail wagging as he ran swiftly from one place to the next, he must have looked like he was playing a game with his handler.

One of them eventually exploded with horrific consequences

But of course this was a very dangerous game, and although many hundreds of mines were found and safely dealt with by Ricky and the other dogs, one of them eventually exploded, with horrific consequences.

The blast killed the soldier who was in charge, and Ricky (who was working only a couple of metres away) received a bad wound to his head. From the size of the crater it left, the force of the explosion must have been enormous, and even without sustaining an injury most dogs would have panicked and run away. But Ricky stayed where he was, close to the other soldiers, and after the noise of the blast died away he got straight back to work. All the men knew they were surrounded by unexploded mines, and Ricky found several more of them before he was taken away to have his wounds cleaned and patched up.

Happily, he made a full recovery, although it took a while before he was fit enough to be back at work. Having seen for themselves how good Ricky was at sniffing out danger, and how brave he was in a crisis, the army tried hard to buy him when the war finally came to an end. Mrs Litchfield refused to change her mind, however, and reminded everyone that the army's dog was actually her pet. Accepting that Ricky had only been lent to them, not donated, the army reluctantly agreed to let him go and, after being collected from the barracks by Mrs Litchfield, Ricky returned home to Kent, where he enjoyed a long and well-earned rest.

CHER AMI: A DARING FLIGHT INTO DANGER

Meuse-Argonne Offensive, First World War, France, 1918

The fittest dog can run only a few kilometres, but a good racing pigeon will fly a hundred kilometres or more to get home. Birds like Cher Ami can even find their way back after setting off from somewhere they have never been before, although on particularly long flights they might lose up to a third of their body weight from all the effort.

How the pigeons navigate such huge distances is something we don't really understand, but it is a mysterious skill which armies have depended on for thousands of years. From Julius Caesar to the 'Iron Duke' of Wellington, history's greatest military commanders have used birds to carry news of their victories. More recently birds such as Cher Ami have been sent by ordinary soldiers with messages warning of death or disaster.

The name Cher Ami is French and means 'Dear Friend', but she was actually an English bird, one of many thousands which were lent or donated to the army at the start of the war by pigeon racers (known as 'fanciers'). Today one of the most famous fanciers in the world is Queen Elizabeth II, and among those who provided champion race-winning birds to help troops fighting overseas were her father, George VI, and her grandfather, George V.

Birds like Cher Ami were vital. A century ago telephone and radio equipment was unreliable even when it wasn't in a waterlogged trench (and when the operator wasn't being shot at). The so-called 'pigeon post' was therefore an invaluable way of sending messages over huge distances and at speeds of up to one hundred kilometres an hour.

The pigeon post was an invaluable way of sending messages over huge distances

It seems incredible that an animal, any animal, can travel this fast. It is extraordinary too to think that a creature as small as Cher Ami would display the kind of courage needed to fly through the smoke, shellfire and explosions of a battle when many much bigger ones would run for cover.

Because of these remarkable abilities there were soon a hundred thousand birds like her flying messages back and forth across the battlefields.

The enemy quickly realised what was going on, and began ordering troops to shoot them down. Attempts were also made to stop the messages being delivered by using hawks or falcons specially trained to bring the pigeons down before they could reach England.

Cher Ami carried her messages in a tiny metal tube attached to her leg, each message kept as short as possible to save weight. Many of them are still officially top secret so it is unknown what they said, but others were SOS or distress messages from troops stranded behind enemy lines or otherwise in danger.

During the course of the war Cher Ami carried many different messages, but the most important one was an SOS from a large group of American soldiers who went missing during one of the last big battles of 1918. Around two hundred soldiers of the 77th Division were fighting in the Argonne Forest in northern France. Heavily outnumbered by German forces, they eventually found themselves pinned down by shellfire and unable to move.

They eventually found themselves pinned down by shellfire and unable to move

The Americans couldn't shoot their way out because they had run out of ammunition. Many of the men had also been wounded in the fighting, but with no medical supplies there was no way to treat them. As the day wore on and the shelling got heavier and heavier, the trapped men realised that they were coming under attack not only from the enemy but from soldiers on their own side who had failed to recognise them.

Night brought a slight lull in the fighting but by the second day their situation was even more desperate and the men were becoming increasingly frightened. They had a few carrier pigeons with them, and so a message was attached to one of the birds and sent off to the battalion HQ. The message read: 'Many wounded. We cannot escape.' But unfortunately the bird was shot down almost as soon as it took off. A second message was written out and attached to another bird – 'Men are suffering. Can support not be sent?' – but again the same thing happened.

The men realised they now had just one pigeon left: Cher Ami. A third, slightly longer message was written out for her to take, explaining exactly where the men were hiding and begging the other American platoons to stop firing on them. This was carefully rolled up into the small metal canister, and clipped to Cher Ami's leg.

All the men knew that this one bird represented their only hope of rescue. The enemy soldiers would have known it too, or at least they might have guessed that, having

All the men knew that this one bird represented their only hope of rescue

run out of ammunition, the Americans would soon run out of pigeons. Because of this, as she rose into the air, Cher Ami was met by a hail of bullets. Even without this, the noise and smoke of battle would have been a terrifying thing for any animal to experience.

No one could be certain at the time, but from where the men were hiding it looked like she'd been hit almost as soon as she left their trench. One wing appeared to dip slightly, Cher Ami slowed and dropped a little, but then she recovered herself and climbed higher and higher above the waiting men before heading for home. In barely an hour the little bird managed to fly more than forty kilometres out of the forest, eventually swooping down to safety behind the lines.

Completely exhausted by her terrifying ordeal, Cher Ami was also badly injured with a broken wing, damage to one eye and part of a leg missing. She still had the all-important message, however, and once this was unrolled and read a rescue mission was hastily launched to bring back what became known as the 'Lost Battalion'. Cher Ami was meanwhile carefully nursed back to health by army medical staff, and even fitted with a miniature wooden leg before being awarded two special medals by the grateful American and French forces.

TICH: A TOUGH FRONT-LINE FIGHTER
Operation Olive, Second World War, Italy, 1945

In 1941 in Egypt a scruffy stray called Tich spotted some soldiers belonging to the King's Royal Rifle Corps and decided to tag along with them.

The men were from England but had travelled all the way to Egypt to fight a huge German invasion force which was threatening the people of north Africa. When they arrived the little mongrel – a bit lonely perhaps, and probably hungry with no one to look after her – saw the soldiers as a good opportunity to scrounge a decent meal.

A lot of the men liked having the dog around, perhaps because she reminded them of the pets many of them would have left back home. They were happy to share their rations with Tich too, and of course she was happy to eat them. In particular she liked a rifleman called Thomas Walker, and the pair very quickly formed a special bond.

From then on they were inseparable. Walker and his comrades spent over two years fighting in the heat of the desert, eventually defeating the enemy there before moving on to Italy where the fighting continued. Tich went everywhere with them. Many of the battles involved tanks and the massive guns designed to destroy them, but Tich never minded the noise and seemed oblivious to the danger. For her the whole thing was just one big adventure, her favourite habit being to ride on the bonnet of Walker's Jeep. At other times she would climb on top of the platoon's Bren Carrier, a special armoured vehicle with caterpillar tracks which was used to carry a large machine gun into battle.

While they were in Italy Tich gave birth to fifteen lovely little puppies whom she nursed until homes could be found for them. She was desperate to get back onto the Jeep and into battle with Rifleman Walker, however, and before long she could be heard howling like a wolf again through the smoke and gunfire and explosions. This was a sound the other soldiers loved to hear, a real boost to their spirits and a sort of rallying cry whenever they were attacking a well-armed enemy.

She could be heard howling like a wolf again through the smoke and gunfire and explosions

Tich always seemed fearless but, like the men, she faced danger almost every day. During her time with Rifleman Walker she was hurt more than once, mostly just minor injuries – cuts and bruises – although on one occasion she was wounded quite badly and for a while looked like she might not survive.

It happened because Rifleman Walker was an exceptionally brave man, and wherever he went Tich would always follow. Both of them took part in Operation Olive, one of the largest battles ever fought in Italy, when a number of British casualties became trapped in an exposed position. These soldiers were coming under massively heavy fire from the German army, and, knowing they needed urgent medical treatment, Walker set out to rescue them.

Operation Olive was one of the largest battles ever fought in Italy

This put him in great danger, and Tich too when she decided to stay by his side. As their Jeep approached the wounded men the shelling got heavier and heavier, but Walker refused to back off or to find somewhere to take cover. Now, like the men who were injured, he and Tich found themselves stuck out in the open. Somehow none of the shells scored a direct hit on their vehicle, but there were explosions all around them. Walker realised after one especially loud bang that Tich had gone quiet and was lying very still on the bonnet of his vehicle.

From a brief examination he suspected she had a broken nose and he could see many smaller wounds from jagged fragments of metal (called shrapnel) which had been thrown out by the explosion. But a rifleman's duty was always to the wounded men and Walker knew he had to treat them first before worrying about his dog.

Poor little Tich turned out to be very badly battered, and when they got her back to safety many of the soldiers were worried that their faithful friend might not recover. After treating the men, Rifleman Walker did his best to patch her up. Once this was done all he and his pals could do was to wait and to hope for the best.

Fortunately, mongrels are famously tough and Tich was certainly no exception. After two or three days' rest, and some attention from the men, she seemed to bounce back. Another few days and she was her usual cheerful self, sporting a few new scars but nothing else to worry about.

The soldiers in Walker's platoon were overjoyed at this and one of them mentioned the story to a reporter who was covering the war for a newspaper back in England. He took a photograph of Tich and sent it to London. With everyone desperate for good news, the newspaper editor decided to publish the photograph beneath a headline describing Tich as 'the brave dog of an outstandingly brave man'.

Tich's toughness and determination had boosted the spirits of everyone around her

In the same piece Walker's commanding officer explained how Tich's toughness and determination had boosted the spirits of everyone around her. The courage and devotion of the little dog, he said, had meant a huge amount to the soldiers, and they had all been cheered by the sight of her. As her master drove through the mayhem to rescue the injured men, the sight and sound of Tich howling away on the Jeep's bonnet must have been fantastic.

The newspaper story made Tich famous, and of course Rifleman Walker was utterly determined to bring her to England when the war was over.

Unsurprisingly, they arrived home to a hero's welcome, and when it was announced that Rifleman Walker was going to be awarded a medal for his courage it was agreed his companion should get one too. The presentation was made at London's famous Wembley Stadium, after which Tich went to live with Walker and his family in Newcastle. She might not have gone on to experience anything as exciting as riding on a Jeep or a Bren Carrier, but despite her injuries Tich lived to be an old dog – and one who was much loved.

APPOLLO: A BRIGHT LIGHT ON THE DARKEST DAY
Ground Zero, New York, 2001

In September 2001, when terrorists crashed two airliners into the World Trade Center in New York, it was immediately clear that emergency teams would be working to recover victims, not rescuing survivors.

The destruction of the famous twin towers was total, and so sudden that there was no chance that any of the two thousand eight hundred people trapped in the buildings would be found alive. The rescue squads knew this but recognised that it was nevertheless vital that they search the ruins thoroughly. Everyone involved wanted to know what had happened on that terrible day, and for bereaved families to hold funerals for their loved ones and pay their respects, the victims' bodies had to be recovered and returned.

In the aftermath of what came to be known as 9/11 nearly three hundred search-and-rescue dogs were brought in to help with this massive task. A few, including an Alsatian named Appollo, were part of New York's own K-9 Dog Unit. Others were brought in from elsewhere in America, many of them spending up to sixteen hours a day searching the site we call Ground Zero.

Nearly three hundred search-and-rescue dogs were brought in to help with this massive task

Appollo was almost certainly the first to arrive as he and his handler, New York police officer Peter Davis, were there within minutes of the disaster. Aged nearly ten, Appollo was quite an old dog but his energy and enthusiasm were as good as ever. He was also one of the most highly trained dogs in America, and had previously done all sorts of different jobs, including search and rescue, weapons recovery, routine patrol work, and even learning the techniques needed to bring down an armed man. His years of experience made him the perfect choice for such a gruelling task, although in the first few hours it's possible that no one realised quite how hazardous the work was going to be.

We now know that the brave men and women in the rescue teams faced all sorts of unseen dangers while clambering over the wreckage. The same was true for Appollo and the other dogs, who, if anything, took even greater risks. Fires were still burning fiercely long after the buildings had collapsed, and for days the air was thick with choking dust and poisonous fumes. At the same time the ruins were so unstable that every step the dogs took carried with it the risk of pitching them down into the deep basements beneath the fallen buildings.

Appollo was oblivious to the dangers and determined to do the best possible job

Within moments of Officer Davis leading him onto the smoking ruins, Appollo knew what was expected of him and was soon working uninterrupted for many hours, moving at speed over the ruins and concentrating on finding the scent of victims in among the smoke and fumes of the wrecked towers. Unsurprisingly the men and women involved would sometimes just stop, completely overwhelmed by the carnage and understandably shocked by it. But Appollo and the other dogs just put their heads down and got on with the task in hand, apparently oblivious to the dangers and determined to do the best possible job.

In particular Appollo showed himself to be an expert when it came to navigating the wreckage of the two buildings. Crossing narrow, makeshift pathways of twisted beams, many of them lying over burning voids many metres below, he missed his footing only once when some rubble gave way beneath his front paws. As he scrabbled to stay upright bright flames shot up around him, but he somehow managed to regain his footing and, refusing to panic, made his way to another part of the great mountain of glass and steel. Unfortunately, as he resumed the search, he slipped through an area of loose debris and landed with a splash in a deep pool of contaminated black water which had collected below.

Appollo quickly scrambled out, but it must have been a shock, although the soaking he received probably saved his life. Less than a minute later he was caught again as yet more flames shot up from the depths, but, with his dog's fur wet through, Officer Davis was able to sweep the burning embers from his coat before he suffered any injuries. Once more Appollo refused to panic at this brush with death, and moments later he was back at work searching the ground around him.

With similar incidents happening all the time it didn't take the authorities long to appreciate how dangerous the work was. They also began to realise how long it was going to take to search literally millions of tons of rubble. Appollo and the other dogs were going to be needed on the site for many months, and so it was important to do something to safeguard them while they went about their work.

> Hundreds of sets of protective doggy boots were soon brought to the site

Hundreds of sets of protective doggy boots were soon brought to the site, many of them made at home by ordinary Americans desperate to do something to help. Mobile veterinary hospitals were also established around the site to care for Appollo and the others, with volunteer vets on hand to examine each animal at the end of its shift, to check coats, eyes and noses for damage from the smoke and dust.

Over the course of many months' work only two dogs had to be sent home as a result of these checks, which is quite surprising. All the men and women working at Ground Zero were provided with masks, breathing apparatus and special protective clothing, but Appollo and his pals were expected to push their noses right down into the contaminated debris and to keep doing this day after day.

Inevitably the strain of doing this eventually showed in some of them. Several search dogs died earlier than might have been expected, perhaps as a result of the stress of the work and the effects of breathing in toxic fumes. Others seemed to suffer emotionally too, and at least one handler noted how, at the end of a long shift, his dog seemed to withdraw into his own small world.

At one point, Officer Davis was similarly concerned that Appollo was beginning to suffer. He thought he might be frustrated by the work, and unhappy at not finding anyone alive whom he could rescue. In an attempt to help, Officer Davis asked a fireman to hide in the wreckage so that Appollo could 'discover' him. It was a simple enough trick, and it worked like a charm. When Appollo appeared to find the fireman everyone made a special fuss of him, and he returned to his work with as much enthusiasm as he had shown on the first day.

To everyone who saw Appollo after that, the message must have seemed clear enough: dogs like him want to help, and want to feel they are helping, but sometimes they need a little help themselves in order to keep going.

Of course many of the dogs at Ground Zero fulfilled another very important role as well, besides finding the victims of this huge tragedy. Nothing beats a dog's nose when it comes to sensitivity and precision, but animal lovers know there's nothing quite like a dog's heart either, and time and again these hard-working and courageous creatures were seen comforting rescue workers as they went about their tasks.

For example, several witnesses reported seeing a golden retriever called Bretagne comforting a fire-fighter at Ground Zero who was in distress. Other rescue workers instinctively sought out the company of one of the dogs whenever they were able to snatch a few minutes' rest. Their work was hard and unrelenting, but we all know how relaxing it is to spend a few minutes stroking a dog, and how spending time with a friendly animal helps us unwind.

Looking back now we can see how Appollo and the other three hundred dogs did so much more than simply search for victims. It's true that on this occasion they were unable to save any lives, because there were no survivors to rescue. But by just being there they provided comfort and support to thousands of fire-fighters and other professionals brought in to work in truly terrible conditions, men and women who might otherwise have cracked under the pressure.

As one rescue worker put it when the work was finally completed: 'If these dogs only knew what a difference they make.'

CHINDIT MINNIE:
BORN IN THE HEAT OF BATTLE
Burma Campaign, Second World War, South-east Asia, 1944

In 1943, in one of the most remarkable episodes of the Second World War, more than twelve thousand men, one thousand three hundred and fifty animals, and hundreds of tons of guns and ammunition were secretly flown more than two hundred and forty kilometres behind enemy lines.

Operating deep in the jungles of Burma the men were known as the Chindits, a secret 'phantom army' made up of British and Commonwealth soldiers who were sent to fight a much larger Japanese invasion force. There was no real hope at this stage of driving the invaders out of the country, but covering more than a thousand kilometres on foot, and living for months right under their noses, the soldiers were able to mount repeated surprise attacks on their camps and bases before melting back into the jungle.

The soldiers were able to mount repeated surprise attacks on their camps and bases

Conditions were truly terrible, and the fighting was ferocious. Everything had to be carried by the men themselves or on the backs of mules, so progress through the jungle was incredibly slow. Occasionally food and medical supplies would be parachuted in, but there was never enough to go round, and as many men fell ill from malnutrition and disease as were injured in the fighting.

You can imagine, then, that on the rare occasions when something nice happened in one of their jungle camps everybody wanted to know about it. The birth of Minnie was definitely one of these occasions, especially as nobody had even realised that one of the pack ponies they were using to carry supplies was pregnant.

No one can remember the pony's name now, but Minnie's mother gave birth during one of the worst periods of fighting in an area known as the White City. The enemy had just launched a prolonged and determined attack and, with mortar bombs raining all round them, the soldiers couldn't believe what they were seeing when a spindly-legged little foal suddenly appeared in their midst.

The timing was clearly awful, but at the same time it must have seemed a bit wonderful as well. Seeing Minnie as a little miracle of life in

A little miracle of life in all the chaos and destruction

all the chaos and destruction, the soldiers were determined to make sure she was all right. As soon as there was a lull in the fighting they all gathered round Minnie and her exhausted mother, offering them water bottles and speaking softly so as not to alarm the new arrival.

Minnie was obviously too small to be used to carry supplies like the other ponies, but in any case the soldiers decided she was too special for that. As news of her arrival travelled down the lines of men camped out in the jungle, more and more of them came over to see the miracle for themselves.

Minnie was soon taking sugar lumps from the men, and learned to drink tea from a pot, which everyone found hugely amusing. Minnie seemed to like making the men laugh, and if something she did got this response she would do it again straight away. She also seemed not to mind the sound of mortars and bombs going off all around her, perhaps because that was the noise which greeted her when she first came into the world.

While the other animals would attempt to stampede whenever a shell fell near them, Minnie would just keep her head down and wait for the noise and hullabaloo to die down. Only once was she at all disturbed by gunfire, which was when a shell fell near a line of mules and one of them, panicked by the noise, kicked out and caught her just below one eye with a hoof.

The injury she received on that occasion was serious, and for a while there was concern among the men that she might lose her sight in that eye. By this time they had been fighting non-stop for almost three months, but every soldier waited with bated breath to hear news about how Minnie was doing. When it was eventually announced that she had completely recovered there were whoops of joy from the men almost as if they had won the war!

In fact there was still a long way to go before the enemy was beaten. It required the exhausted men to march north, even deeper into the jungle, and as they prepared to do this it was decided that it was too dangerous to risk taking Minnie along.

Plans were hatched to fly her out of the jungle and on to somewhere safe

Most of the soldiers agreed with this, but it left them with a major problem about what to do with their little mascot. The Chindits understood why they couldn't take Minnie with them, but they knew they couldn't leave her behind either. For them she wasn't just a pony but an important symbol of their survival, and so plans were hatched to fly her out of the jungle and on to somewhere safe.

Doing this was going to be very dangerous: it required an aeroplane to be flown deep into enemy territory, land, take off and then fly out again without being spotted. Attempting such a feat also broke just about every law of military discipline, endangering men and machines for the sake of an animal. Decades later it sounds like a huge risk to have taken, but thousands of kilometres away in the jungle the men all loved their Minnie and knew what had to be done.

A number of officers agreed to turn a blind eye while a rescue plan was put into operation. Minnie had to be readied for the journey so that she could be loaded on to the plane as soon as it landed. It was important to get it turned around and sent on its way as quickly as possible, and before the enemy realised what was going on.

Happily, the plan worked like clockwork. Almost as soon as the landing strip was cleared an aeroplane was heard over the treetops. It swooped down, taxied to a halt, and within just a minute or two the little pony was loaded on board and bound for India. The men were sad to see her go, but as anxious eyes watched the aircraft with its precious cargo climb slowly towards the clouds they must have known she would be safer.

Within a few hours Minnie had landed at a military base in British India and been greeted as a celebrity. By the time the Chindits made it back from the jungle a few months later she was entirely at home in her new surroundings. She still drank tea from a pot, and would nibble tablecloths and steal food if she thought it would make the men laugh. Like the phantom army, Minnie had been through her fair share of hardship, and now, for those who had survived the war, she represented the joy of life.

For those who had survived the war, she represented the joy of life

PRINCE: THE DOG
WHO RAN AWAY TO WAR
The Western Front, First World War, northern France, 1914

Prince was a small Irish terrier, a slightly shaggy mutt who belonged to Private James Brown, a soldier in the North Staffordshire Regiment.

Private Brown and his comrades were among the first troops to be sent to France when war was declared against Germany in 1914. At that time everyone expected the fighting to be over quickly, with many of the soldiers looking forward to the adventure and assuming they would be back home by Christmas.

Prince may have thought so too, but as weeks passed, and the war dragged on, at home in London the once lively little dog missed his master terribly. As the weeks became months he seemed to lose his spark. As a puppy he had always been mischievous and playful, but now he just lay around the house all day, eating almost nothing and refusing to go out. If Prince heard the front door he would run to see if it was his master, home at last. Each time it wasn't, poor Prince would look even more miserable than he had before.

The rest of the family loved Prince and tried hard to cheer him up with games and treats – but nothing seemed to work. One morning they were alarmed to find Prince was missing. For months he had refused to leave the house, but now he had escaped through an open door or window and was nowhere to be seen. Asking friends and neighbours to help, the family spent all day searching the streets in their part of London, but as night began to fall they realised that Prince really had vanished and might never be found.

Prince really had vanished and might never be found

No one wanted to pass on the bad news, but Mrs Brown knew that eventually she must write to her husband and tell him about his dog. By now the regiment was fighting hard in France. Soldiers were coming under heavy bombardment nearly every day, with shells exploding over the trenches and snipers firing at them whenever anyone stuck his head above the parapet. Knowing her husband would be under terrible stress, Mrs Brown chose her words carefully, but there was no disguising the sadness in her letter: Private Brown's special little dog had disappeared.

After a couple of weeks she had heard nothing from France so she decided to write again. This time she got a reply, a short handwritten note from Private Brown telling her not to worry about the dog. Prince was alive and well, it said, and living with his regiment in France!

How the pair found each other is an incredible story, but one which no one can fully explain. James Brown had been staying in a village close to the battlefield when he spotted a dog that looked just like the one he had left behind in London. Although he was in another country he called out Prince's name out of habit, and was astonished when the little dog appeared to jump up in surprise, spin round and then run full-pelt towards him.

Private Brown couldn't believe it but this really was his dog. Prince was beside himself with excitement and was soon running round and round his master and in and out of his legs. When Brown bent down to pat him Prince leapt up to lick his face, each of them as happy as the other.

The chances of the two meeting in this way, so far from home, must have been tiny. To get there Prince would have had to find his way across London, down to the coast and over the English Channel. Even then he would have to have travelled more than one hundred kilometres through war-torn France and somehow arrived in the very same village his master was staying in.

The chances of the two meeting in this way, so far from home, must have been tiny

No one could imagine how a little dog managed to do all this on its own, but a hundred years later it is possible to make a guess. For example, we know that the men of a second British regiment, called the Queen's Westminsters, were in London at the time Prince vanished and that they too were bound for France. Prince might have seen them and run up to them, thinking he would find his master among all these men in uniform. Everyone who knew Prince said he was always a very friendly dog so the soldiers probably enjoyed having him around. Maybe one of them decided to smuggle the cheerful scamp on to the ship taking them to France.

However he got there, through all the fighting and the horror, the little dog's arrival and his happy reunion with Private Brown were greeted as a miracle by many of the soldiers. A rare bit of good news at a time when the war was going badly, the story quickly travelled up and down the trenches. Soon more and more of the men came by to see the little terrier for themselves, and within days of his arrival Prince was being treated like a celebrity.

Even so, a muddy, waterlogged trench in wartime was no place for a pet. When Private Brown's commanding officer heard about the dog he wasn't pleased at all. He insisted on seeing Prince for himself, however, and when he did he could see that having him around was good for morale. Because of this he agreed the dog could stay with his troops, and share their rations.

When the men were marching Prince definitely kept their spirits up by running alongside them and playing around. After overcoming his natural fear of exploding shells Prince also helped during the fighting, especially by providing real comfort and company for any wounded soldiers waiting to be rescued and taken back home.

Prince provided real comfort and company for any wounded soldiers

Before long Prince was officially adopted as the North Staffordshires' very special regimental mascot. He never got as close to the other soldiers as he was to Private Brown, but over the next four years he proved a good friend to so many of them that when the war ended in 1918 the army didn't want to let him go. Private Brown was keen to get back to his family and was asked if Prince could remain behind with the other soldiers of the regiment. He said no, without hesitation, determined that as true friends the two of them would never again be separated. He and Prince returned to England and to the family they had left behind all those years before.

Daisy: keeping morale afloat

On board a Norwegian trawler, Second World War, North Sea, 1942

With Norway invaded and occupied by German soldiers for much of the Second World War hundreds of courageous Norwegian civilians risked their lives working for the resistance.

For five years these brave men and women attacked the occupying forces whenever they could and wherever they found them. Organising raids to sabotage railways and strategically important bridges, under cover of darkness they would also spy on the enemy's movements and disrupt their plans. Anything interesting was immediately reported back to the British authorities who supplied arms and expertise to help them in the fight.

Many of these people had been ordinary sailors and fishermen before the war, and they now found themselves sailing secretly from Norway to Scotland and back again. They made the crossing many times, rescuing people in Norway who were being hunted by the secret police, and on the return journeys delivering the agents and weapons needed to help liberate their country.

Every trip of this sort was dangerous, and the men knew they would be tried and shot if they were ever caught. Designed for fishing, not fighting, their trawlers were far from perfect, being mostly old, noisy and painfully slow. There was also the ever-present risk of attack from hostile aircraft and submarines, and the crews were constantly on the look-out for danger. To avoid being spotted they had to make as much as possible of each crossing at night, and even then they could only do it if the moon was obscured by clouds, making it dark enough for them to evade detection.

The men knew they would be tried and shot if they were ever caught

On one of these vessels the crew kept a mascot, a lively little mongrel called Daisy. There wasn't much for a dog to do on board a boat so she was probably only there to keep the crew company. Having an animal along would break the monotony of the long trips across the North Sea, and by all accounts Daisy was a friendly dog whom the men all liked.

Despite taking great care to avoid being caught, several of these special trawlers were nevertheless torpedoed and sunk. One winter's night Daisy's boat was spotted by the crew of an enemy vessel and came under attack. Trawlers are slow, so the captain knew he couldn't out-run it. Instead he ordered one of the crew to tap out a brief SOS message giving their position while the others made an effort to return the enemy's fire using a couple of machine guns. Unfortunately, it was no good, and moments later the night sky was briefly illuminated by a sudden, blinding flash as the Norwegian boat was struck by a torpedo.

Several of the sailors were killed outright, and the force of the blast pitched Daisy and the remaining men into the dark, icy sea. The trawler sank in less than a minute. Without a life raft to cling to, the men were left floating around in the darkness. Their only hope was that someone somewhere had heard the SOS and that another boat would soon be on its way to rescue them.

For the men it was to be the longest and most dangerous night of their lives. In the middle of winter the sea was bitterly cold, and they had no way of knowing if help was on its way. If they were to be rescued it was vital that they stay together, and important that each man stayed afloat and didn't drift off into unconsciousness as a result of tiredness and the desperate cold.

Daisy never gave up on her crew and spent the night giving the men as much comfort as she could

As experienced seamen they knew this, and Daisy seemed to sense it too. Through the long dark hours she paddled around the men, helping to keep them together. Constantly moving, and going from one to another, she licked the sailors' faces to keep them awake.

The ordeal must have been just as terrifying for her because dogs don't like freezing water any more than we do, especially in the dark. But Daisy never gave up on her crew and spent the night giving the men as much comfort as she could in bleak and frightening circumstances.

Amazingly, the trawler's distress call had been picked up by someone on the Scottish mainland, and as dawn broke over the North Sea one of the exhausted sailors spotted a rescue vessel making its way towards them. A few minutes later the crew were all hauled aboard, Daisy included. Warm, dry clothes were provided, and something hot to drink, and later that morning they clambered ashore in Scotland.

Describing the attack and its aftermath, the survivors were unanimous in their praise for the trawler's little mascot, and they loved her for it. Many of them would not have lasted the night without Daisy's care and comfort. Similarly, her stubborn refusal to be beaten must have been a powerful inspiration for others in the resistance too, committed as they were to a long hard fight to take back their country.

THEO: THE DOG
WHO DIED OF A BROKEN HEART
Helmand Province, Afghanistan, 2011

A dog trained to detect explosive booby traps in a war zone such as Afghanistan needs to be a hundred per cent accurate and completely reliable. As well as having a sensitive sense of smell, they must also be exceptionally keen because soldiers cannot rely on a dog which loses interest after half an hour or which cannot stand the heat and the noise.

Theo was a lively black and white spaniel who didn't seem to mind the discomforts of desert life, and he was never happier than when he was out working with his handler, Lance Corporal Liam Tasker. The pair were described as inseparable by comrades, and theirs is a sad but very moving story of the friendship which can develop between an animal and a human being.

As part of Britain's 1st Military Working Dog Regiment, Liam and Theo were sent to the most dangerous part of Afghanistan in 2011. They were responsible for locating hidden weapons, bomb-making equipment and improvised explosive devices (or IEDs). Home-made but deadly, these kill and injure many soldiers and civilians every year, so dealing with them is vital but incredibly dangerous.

Both man and dog were exceptionally good at the task, and in a very short time Theo had made fourteen confirmed operational finds. This is still a record for any dog working in Afghanistan, a country where mines and other explosive devices buried in the ground have killed more than one thousand one hundred men, women and children, and injured more than two thousand others.

As well as dealing with the threat of IEDs in this way, Liam and Theo located a cache of equipment used to make much bigger and deadlier bombs too. On one occasion they even discovered a secret tunnel which led to an underground room being used by the enemy. Ordinarily Theo would have been sent home to England after six months, but because he was so good at his work the army decided to extend his tour of duty by an extra few weeks.

It was not unusual for Liam and Theo to go out on two or three patrols a day, and often they would have to carry out their life-saving searches while coming under heavy fire from hidden gunmen. Unfortunately, every now and then one of these enemy snipers managed to get close enough to set up an effective ambush, and on one such occasion twenty-six-year-old Liam was shot while out on patrol with the Irish Guards.

He died instantly and, faithful to his master, Theo stayed by his side. A helicopter rushed them both back to the base, but shortly after it landed, Theo suffered a kind of seizure or heart attack and he too died.

Theo was still only a young dog, less than two years old, and like all military animals he was physically extremely fit. There were no signs of any serious injuries from the ambush, and so his death seemed impossible to explain. Even after examining his body carefully the base vets couldn't understand what had happened, but hearing the story many animal lovers soon reached their own sad conclusion. After losing Liam, they say, his companion, his comrade and his best friend, Theo had simply died of a broken heart.

After working together so courageously they died true heroes

For everyone who knew them it was a terrible, terrible tragedy. Described by senior officers as a rising star, Liam was recognised by all his fellow soldiers as a brave man who day after day carried out one of the army's most dangerous jobs regardless of the threat to his own life. Where Liam went, Theo was happy to follow, and after working together so courageously they died true heroes.

Liam and Theo are now thought to be buried together near Liam's family home in Scotland, inseparable to the end. Let's hope their story is never forgotten.

G.I. JOE: ONE FLIGHT, A THOUSAND LIVES SAVED
The Battle for Calvi Vecchia, Second World War, Italy, 1943

It's amazing to think that in order to fly more than thirty kilometres in just twenty minutes a bird would need to travel at the sort of speed a car does when it is being driven on a motorway. That's what one army pigeon managed to do in Italy, however, and as a result G.I. Joe is thought to have saved around a thousand British lives.

In October 1943 many hundreds of soldiers from a London regiment were planning to launch an attack on a well-fortified enemy position in

The soldiers were planning to launch an attack on a well-fortified enemy position

the south of the country. For several days heavily armed German troops had barricaded themselves into a town called Calvi Vecchia. The plan was for the American air force to bomb the town first so that the British could march in and capture the defenders.

As the British moved into position, however, they realised that the town had become suspiciously quiet. Looking through powerful binoculars they could see no sign of any movement, and for a while assumed the enemy was planning to ambush them as they attacked. A few soldiers moved even closer to check this out, but then realised the defenders had disappeared. Presumably fearing an attack of the kind the British and Americans were planning, they had withdrawn from the town and melted away into the countryside.

For the soldiers this was naturally a huge relief for it meant they could recapture Calvi Vecchia without firing a shot. But very quickly their relief turned to fear when they realised the Americans were about to start bombing the town in which they were now standing.

The soldiers knew they did not have enough time to get far enough away from the town or to reach a safe position before the bombers arrived. For technical reasons they were also unable to contact the American air force by radio. Fortunately, they had a carrier pigeon with them. As G.I. Joe belonged to the Americans he could be relied on to fly back to them if he was released.

The airfield was more than thirty kilometres away and the soldiers knew the raid was due to start in about twenty minutes. With no time to lose a message was hastily written out, explaining the situation and ordering the raid to be called off. This was then rolled up and inserted into a canister clipped to G.I. Joe's leg, and the bird was released into the air.

To reach the airfield in time Joe would have to average one hundred kilometres per hour, an incredible speed for a pigeon, but just about possible in the right conditions. Of course the soldiers would not be able to see him after the first minute or two, and so all they could do was to hope for the best and pray he got to the Americans before the bombers took off.

To reach the airfield in time Joe would have to average one hundred kilometres per hour

We now know that Joe flew like the wind because he arrived at the American air base with just seconds to spare. The bombers were actually moving into position for take-off when G.I. Joe was spotted, and they would have been airborne moments later. As soon as Joe landed, his message was unrolled and read out, and at the last possible moment the fleet of bombers was ordered to stop.

Joe's heroic flight meant that the town of Calvi Vecchia was saved from destruction, together with the lives of up to a thousand British soldiers who would otherwise have been bombed by their own allies. It was hardly the longest flight of the war, but it was definitely one of the fastest, and the number of lives saved by one bird has never been beaten. After the war G.I. Joe went on to spend a well-earned retirement in America, but in 1946 made a special trip back across the Atlantic when he was awarded a medal at the Tower of London.

SIMON: THE CAT WHO SAVED HIS CREW

The Yangtze Incident, Chinese Civil War, China, 1949

Cats have long been kept on board ship, and those adopted by the Royal Navy have always had to earn their keep. Simon was discovered living wild in Hong Kong in the 1940s, and after being taken on board a visiting British warship, HMS *Amethyst*, he was expected to keep the warship's stores free of the rats and mice which were always trying to steal the sailors' food.

The sailors liked having him around, and the black and white tom spent much of the day curled up asleep in the captain's hat. But at night Simon turned into a ferocious hunter, and most mornings he would leave a row of dead bodies on deck to show how busy he had been. Occasionally a dead mouse would be hidden in one of the sailors' shoes, but as long as their food was safe no one seemed to mind.

In 1949 the *Amethyst* was on patrol one hundred and fifty kilometres up China's mighty Yangtze River. She had been sent there not to fight but to protect Britons living in China during its long and bloody civil war. Unfortunately she became caught up in a fierce battle between the two warring sides: Communist troops firing from one side of the river and Nationalist soldiers firing from the other.

She became caught up in a fierce battle between the two warring sides

The first few shells passed harmlessly overhead, but then one smashed down onto the *Amethyst*, blowing a huge hole in the side. The captain was killed in the blast, and several of the sailors badly injured.

Over the next hour many more shells hit the ship, damaging one engine and then wrecking the ship's generator. An SOS message was sent by radio to other Royal Navy vessels in the area, saying the ship was now disabled and could not move. By this time Simon had disappeared, and more than a dozen men lay dead. Many more were injured, and the situation for everyone on board looked extremely serious.

The British were determined not to become involved in the fighting, but if any of the sailors attempted to abandon ship or move around on deck they were met by deadly volleys of gunfire from snipers on the riverbank.

More worryingly, the ship was sinking slowly despite the crew's efforts to plug the jagged holes left by more than fifty shells. Supplies of food were also very low, and, with no sign of Simon, the ship's galley, where they prepared the meals, was soon overrun by rats.

The SOS message had been picked up by another ship belonging to the Royal Navy, and before long it was steaming up the river to attempt a rescue. But as it neared the *Amethyst* it too came under fire, and following the deaths of another nine sailors it was decided to abandon the attempt to tow the *Amethyst* to safety and the rescue ship withdrew.

It was decided to abandon the attempt to tow the *Amethyst* to safety

Simon, it turned out, had been injured in the blast that killed the captain and, as wounded animals often do, he had gone off to find somewhere quiet to lick his wounds and recover. After a few hours he emerged from his hiding place looking scared and a bit dishevelled. He made straight for the sickbay, where some of the more seriously wounded sailors were being treated. It was almost as if he knew that his loud purring and friendly nature would comfort the sailors, and he spent much of the day jumping from bed to bed.

Simon kept this up for the next few weeks, but refused to let it interfere with his other duties. His nocturnal hunting expeditions were now going to be more important than ever, with the sailors' meals severely rationed in order to save what little food was left on board. Simon seemed to understand this straight away, and he was soon catching mice and rats in such huge numbers that the sailors began to keep score.

Most of them couldn't believe how hard Simon was working,

particularly as he was still suffering from the effects of the initial blast. A number of shell fragments had been removed from his little body, and when his whiskers grew back they were badly bent. But despite this his score went up and up as Simon fought to bring the rodent problem under control.

Simon fought to bring the rodent problem under control

Simon's skill as a hunter was important, and not just because the food was running out. It also helped raise morale among the men. They had been trapped now for nearly three months, and had lost several comrades in the attacks. Simon seemed to be waging a small war on their behalf, and what's more he was winning. The sailors were especially pleased when he appeared one morning holding a particularly large and ugly dead rat by the tail. As a reward it was decided to promote him to Able Seaman Simon – making him a real sailor, like the rest of them.

The crew knew they had to escape, however, because even Simon could not prevent the food running out eventually. The next very dark night, with fuel and supplies running dangerously low, it was decided to cut the *Amethyst* loose from her moorings in the hope the ship could drift downriver without being seen. The plan worked, and after floating out of the danger zone the battle-scarred ship was then towed to safety by another Royal Navy vessel which had been sent to meet her.

The crew's ordeal had lasted a total of a hundred and one days, but when they reached the safety of Hong Kong harbour it was finally over. The crew received a personal message from King George VI, and when the story was reported in the

Even Simon could not prevent the food running out eventually

newspapers several members of the public sent money to buy Able Seaman Simon fresh fish and pots of cream. The Royal Navy made him a gift too, a special medal ribbon for his collar to say thank you for his courage, good service and faithfulness to his comrades.

It took another few weeks for the crew to make it back to Britain, and when they did they were welcomed home by the prime minister. As the hero of the *Amethyst* Simon should have been there too, but unfortunately he was in quarantine, a period of isolation needed to ensure that animals from abroad don't bring back any dangerous diseases. Sadly, while there he died, despite still being quite a young cat.

The likelihood is that his injuries had left Simon too weak to fight off any infections, and he must have missed the shipmates he had done so much to help. His heroism had not gone unnoticed, however, and thousands of people sent flowers, and letters and cards saying how sad they were. Of course no one was sadder than Simon's shipmates, and they arranged for the coffin to be covered in the Union Jack and for Britain's most famous cat to be buried with full military honours.

TIPPERARY BEAUTY:
THE DOG WHO RESCUED PETS
The Blitz, Second World War, London, 1940

People weren't the only victims of the Blitz. Thousands of animals were injured or made homeless by the air raids on London in the 1940s.

Many were pets abandoned by families who had been bombed out of their homes, but there were working animals, too. These included the horses used to pull carts and cabs around the capital, and even cows which were still kept in London to provide fresh supplies of milk.

The main rescue efforts always concentrated on finding people trapped in buildings, but a charity called the People's Dispensary for Sick Animals (PDSA) organised volunteer rescue squads to locate and treat injured animals after each air raid. These PDSA squads had a small fleet of old ambulances, and special hospitals where pets and other animals could be fed and looked after.

One of the volunteers was Bill Barnett, who had a pet terrier called Tipperary Beauty (or Beauty for short). Beauty had an exceptionally keen sense of smell, and she soon demonstrated a real knack for sniffing out the sort of places where cats and dogs could be found after an air raid.

Many other animals were trapped in collapsed or burning buildings

Some might just have been hiding, understandably terrified by the loud whistling sound of the bombs falling and then exploding. Like some pets during a thunderstorm, they were probably just desperate to find a safe place to hide until it was all over. But many other animals were trapped in collapsed or burning buildings, or were injured in the fires and by falling debris.

Finding them became Beauty's favourite thing to do, and from the start she was brilliant at it. No one had trained her for this kind of work as she was just an ordinary pet dog. And no one was more surprised than Bill when one day she started pawing away at a pile of rubble and wouldn't leave it alone.

Because she wouldn't stop Bill thought he ought to investigate. He grabbed a shovel, and after a few minutes hard digging the two of them had managed to make a hole large enough for a frightened little cat to crawl out of from under a broken kitchen table. Beauty had always liked to accompany Bill down to the air-raid shelter whenever the bombs started falling. Now, as soon as the raid stopped, she would bound back up the steps and out into the street to look for another pet to rescue.

The rescue of a much-loved pet was often a real comfort

Bill always insisted that what he was doing was just as important as the work done by the teams looking for injured people, and Beauty seemed to feel the same way. After all, no one likes to think of animals going missing or getting hurt, and the rescue of a much-loved pet was often a real comfort to families who had lost their homes in the bombing.

It was also important to locate any missing animals as quickly as possible, and Beauty was better at it and much faster than any of the rescue squad members. She was energetic, nimble and keen to get searching as soon as she could; a building might be smouldering, or even on fire, but Beauty would always rush straight in.

Her courage in doing this meant she risked injuring herself, and so Bill had two pairs of little leather boots specially made for her. He knew he couldn't stop Beauty running into dangerous buildings to start sniffing around, but at least this way her paws would be protected from being burnt or cut by jagged fragments left by the bombs.

Perhaps the best thing about Beauty, however, was her stubborn refusal to give up if she thought she had found something. All of us get tired, and even the best volunteers occasionally managed to convince themselves they had done everything they could and that it was time to go home. But Beauty never seemed to get tired, and sometimes when everyone else was packing up to go Bill would realise his dog was still hard at it.

The other thing Bill knew about Beauty was that she was never, ever wrong

After so many rescues together he knew how to recognise the signs that his little friend had found something. It wasn't just her refusal to follow him off the site but also the excited way in which she would paw the ground again and again. She wasn't big enough to dig through great piles of brick and stone, but she knew Bill and his mates could. Because of this she would keep going until they came to help her, something which never took long because the other thing Bill knew about Beauty was that she was never, ever wrong.

WHITE VISION: A FLYING BIRD ON A FLYING BOAT

RAF coastal patrols, Second World War, off the Scottish coast, 1943

Many thousands of birds took to the air during the Second World War but did so using wings other than their own. These were homing pigeons belonging to the Royal Air Force, a means of ensuring that, wherever they were, bomber crews in trouble could send an emergency message back to their home base.

Aircraft were of course fitted with radios for pilots to communicate with each other and their airfields, but these were not always reliable. Equipment would malfunction, the radio wouldn't work if the aircraft ditched in the sea, and a pilot who crash-landed behind enemy lines would not want to use a radio if this would give away his position to the enemy.

Because of this two birds were supplied with each aircraft. If the crew got into trouble SOS messages could be sent up with the birds in the hope that they would fly back to base so that the men could be rescued.

In October 1943 this happened to the eleven-man crew of a Royal Air Force Catalina flying boat, an aircraft that could land on water. As part of RAF Coastal Command, the men were based more than one hundred and sixty kilometres north of mainland Scotland in the Shetland Isles. Often flying in exceptionally poor weather, their job involved searching many kilometres out to sea for enemy submarines known as U-boats, and on board they carried two pigeons, one of whom was called White Vision.

These men would typically spend more than twenty hours in the air at a stretch, so it was exhausting work. The two birds were kept in specially made boxes, complete with a supply of food and water. But the Catalina was cold and uncomfortable for the men, although with its long-range fuel tanks, powerful machine guns and up to two thousand kilograms of bombs it was very well equipped for hunting submarines.

This particular Catalina had been flying non-stop for twenty-one hours when disaster struck

This particular Catalina had been flying non-stop for twenty-one hours when disaster struck. The weather had been stormy for most of the previous day and night, but now turned really nasty. Unable to land on one of the

Scottish islands, Flying Officer R. W. G. Vaughan was ordered to fly south to Aberdeen. This was well over two hundred and fifty kilometres away, but as the weather continued to worsen he was redirected again, this time to Oban, another two hundred and twenty-five kilometres away.

Weather conditions were no better in Oban either, and with his fuel running out, FO Vaughan took the decision to ditch the plane in the sea. Ordinarily this would not have been a problem: Catalinas were designed for just such a manoeuvre. But in a big storm like this one there was always a risk that an aircraft would capsize or break up. Because of this Vaughan knew he had to send a distress call as quickly as possible.

As soon as the aircraft splashed down the radio failed, perhaps because some water had got into the works. The crew quickly took the two pigeons from their containers. Messages were attached to their legs saying where the aircraft had come down, and then both were released into the storm. Pigeons don't like flying in bad weather, or out at sea, but after circling the plane a couple of times both birds headed off.

As well as pigeons, each RAF Catalina carried two inflatable life rafts for emergencies like this one. Vaughan decided the men should get clear of the flying boat as quickly as possible in case it began to sink. Unfortunately, conditions were becoming so rough that when one of the rafts was launched it was blown further out to sea when only two of the men had climbed into it. Because the second raft was too small to accommodate the other nine crew members, a decision was taken for all of them to stay on the plane for as long as possible.

With the Catalina likely to break up or sink in the storm, the birds were now their only hope of survival

With the Catalina likely to break up or sink in the storm, the birds were now their only hope of survival. Unfortunately, the storm also made things far more dangerous for the birds too, and with the wind and rain becoming fiercer and fiercer the first bird the crew sent off was never to be seen again. It's impossible to be sure exactly what happened, but she was probably beaten back by gale-force winds, in which case she would have fallen, exhausted, into the sea and drowned.

Despite low cloud and very poor visibility White Vision somehow found her way back to land after an amazing nine hours in the air

The men couldn't have known this either of course, but luckily the second bird, White Vision, fared rather better. Despite low cloud and very poor visibility she somehow found her way back to land after an amazing nine hours in the air. Storm-battered, exhausted and with many of her once-white feathers torn away by the force of the weather, she returned to her loft, where the message was quickly unfurled and read.

By this time the wrecked Catalina had been drifting for nearly half a day, meaning the crew were now many kilometres from the position they had been in when Vaughan sent up the birds. No one knew quite how far they would have travelled, but rough calculations based on wind speed, tidal drift and the bird's arrival time enabled RAF personnel to make a reasonable guess. A fast boat was sent out to search a wide area of sea.

It took a while, mostly because the weather was still so poor, but nearly two days after Vaughan's desperate decision to ditch the stricken Catalina the men were finally spotted. Time now really was running out, and within just moments of the last man being pulled clear of the poor old aircraft it broke up and disappeared beneath the waves. The two men who had disappeared on the first life raft were located shortly afterwards, and by the time the launch made it back to dry land White Vision was being hailed as a hero.

Having saved eleven airmen's lives she was renamed White Saviour and, relieved of any further flying duties, she went on to enjoy a long and well-earned retirement.

SHEILA: BRAVING BLIZZARDS TO GET A CREW HOME

A deadly plane crash, Second World War, northern England, 1944

A decorated soldier in the First World War, John Dagg had returned home to the wild Cheviot Hills on the border of England and Scotland. In 1944 he was working as a shepherd in this beautiful but remote landscape, accompanied everywhere by his collie Sheila.

Many of the most beautiful parts of the country get the worst weather, and the Cheviots are no exception. Even on a perfect day the hills are difficult to navigate on foot, and the weather can change in an instant, reducing visibility to near zero and making it easy to get lost.

Even on a perfect day the hills are difficult to navigate on foot

In December 1944 a United States Army Air Force bomber was flying back from a raid when it ran into a blizzard. The immense silver Boeing B-17G Flying Fortress was piloted by Lieutenant George A. Kyle, and with the terrible weather making it impossible to return to his home base in Cambridgeshire he was looking for somewhere safe to land.

Lieutenant Kyle had become disorientated after running into the blizzard, and he decided to bring the aircraft down below the clouds so that he and his eight-man crew could try and work out where they were. To do this the B-17 had to fly very low over the snow-covered Cheviots, a range of hills over eight hundred metres high at their peak.

In any conditions the manoeuvre would have been difficult, and the weather only made it worse. Lieutenant Kyle was a skilled and experienced pilot, however, and realising that he was too low he wrestled with the controls to bring the plane's nose back up again. It was too late: unable to gain altitude fast enough, the Flying Fortress ploughed into the ground with a mighty crash, scattering debris everywhere. The point of impact was just beneath the summit of the highest hill, and the stricken bomber slid violently across a patch of peat bog before coming to a halt by a rocky outcrop called Braydon Crag.

The aircraft still had bombs on board, but remarkably none of these exploded. The sound of the crash was nevertheless loud enough to carry

down to the valleys, and it was heard by several local people, including the shepherd John Dagg and his eleven-year-old son (also called John).

The father lost no time in setting out for the hill with his collie Sheila, telling young John to contact the authorities and report what had happened. The crash was too far away for either of them to have seen it even in good weather, but through the blizzard they could hear and smell the fires which had erupted around the bomber's ruptured fuel lines.

With Sheila running on ahead, John Dagg started to make his way towards the scene of the disaster. He knew the landscape well, guessed the crash site must be at least five kilometres from the road, and was prepared for a long and hard climb in the brutal weather.

Even for a fit man like John it was slow going. Over rocks and through heavy snow, Sheila was much faster, and long before her master got anywhere near the wreckage she had already located four of the nine-man crew. Finding them sheltering from the bitter cold in a trench cut into the peat, she ran back to find her master so she could lead him back to where they were lying.

She had already located four of the nine-man crew

When Dagg got there the men were too shocked and dazed to explain what had happened, but they warned him to keep away from the wreckage. By this time the fuselage and four huge engines were burning fiercely, and of course there were still live bombs on board.

Two of the men were clearly injured, so the first thing to do was to administer some basic first aid to them. All four of them were barefoot too, having lost their shoes in the crash, so Dagg helped them to wrap their feet using strips of material cut from a parachute. All this time the blizzard continued to blow, and with the temperature still falling John Dagg decided to lead these four to safety before coming back to look for the others.

With two of the men injured, and the snow getting deeper all the time, the journey back down the hill was painfully slow. Sheila led them down the easiest path she could find, but it was still several hours before the men reached the warmth and safety of the shepherd's little cottage. As they did so a huge explosion ripped through the air. The blast was enough to shatter several windows in the area, suggesting that the flames had finally reached the bombs being carried on the plane.

As the noise echoed across the hills John Dagg's son told him that three more crew members had been found clambering down on their own. They included the badly injured pilot, but it meant two crewmen were still out there somewhere. Though visibly exhausted after struggling against the elements for more than seven hours, the shepherd turned around and immediately set off back up the hill with his dog. Unsurprisingly, they were soon beaten back by the weather: darkness was falling, and it was simply too dangerous to press on.

Two crewmen were still out there somewhere

At daybreak the next day the two resumed their search, and very quickly found the bodies of two men who had been killed when the nose section of the bomber ploughed into the ground. By now the Flying Fortress was a smoking, burned-out carcass, and there was nothing to do but recover the bodies and head back down to the village.

The story might have ended there, except that the Daggs decided to stay in touch with the airmen and their families after they had returned home to the USA. The shepherd also offered to tend the graves of the two men who had died in the crash and were buried in a nearby cemetery. When the mother of one of them sent a letter to say thank you for this, she also explained how grateful she was for Sheila's help with the rescue. Seeing the letter, John Dagg's son wrote back saying Sheila was now expecting puppies, and would she like one?

It was an irresistible offer and a few months later a little off-white puppy called Tibbie was flown across the Atlantic to a new life in America. The newspapers loved the story: a small but happy footnote to a terrible tragedy. A few months later Tibbie was awarded a prize for 'best-cared-for pet' at a local dog show, making her something of a local celebrity as well as a much-loved family friend.

JET OF IADA: THE DOG THAT LEAPT UP A LADDER
The Blitz, Second World War, London, 1944

Seeing ordinary dogs busy rescuing people and animals from buildings destroyed in the Blitz, the army and RAF realised they ought to train dogs of their own for similar duties.

Jet of Iada was one of the first, a handsome Alsatian from Liverpool who showed a talent for locating people trapped in ruins. In 1944 he

travelled to London with his handler, Corporal Wardle. Despite being sick several times during the journey – Jet always hated travelling in the back of a van or lorry – he rescued his first injured man within minutes of being instructed to search a bombed-out building.

The building was still smoking, so he must have had an extraordinary sense of smell to detect the survivor. This was something he demonstrated again and again, even managing to find people buried deep beneath the rubble of factories full of dangerous chemicals and poisonous smoke.

He must have had an extraordinary sense of smell to detect the survivor

Jet had a knack of knowing where to go, but he was also incredibly brave. Nearly every animal has an instinctive fear of fire, and dogs are no exception. When Jet was on duty, however, he never refused to enter a burning building if he knew this was what Corporal Wardle wanted him to do. Sometimes his handler would have to hold him back, if the flames were too fierce or the building looked like it was going to collapse. But if Wardle felt it was safe to carry on Jet would trust him and rush straight in to begin his search.

During the course of his first year on duty Jet rescued more than a hundred people this way, sometimes after everyone around him had given up. On one occasion the ruins of a hotel had been searched so carefully that the other rescuers were convinced Jet had got it wrong. Various different piles of rubble had been investigated and dug up several times, but Jet was still jumpy and excited. Corporal Wardle knew that meant that he had not finished yet.

Jet seemed particularly interested in a section of wall that was leaning over crazily but had not quite fallen down. When one of the rescuers brought a ladder Jet tried to clamber up it, which was something none of them had seen a dog do before. Eventually one of the men climbed up instead – very carefully, as the ruins were highly unstable – and at the top found an old lady who was trapped on a brick ledge.

One of the men found an old lady who was trapped on a brick ledge

She turned out to be one of the hotel guests and she had been too shocked to cry out. The ledge was also too narrow for her to risk moving in case she slipped and fell. Somehow clever Jet had known where she was, although she was too high above ground for any dog to have picked up her scent.

Although exhausted by her ordeal, and covered in dust and dirt, the lady fortunately went on to make a full recovery. Corporal Wardle never did work out how his dog had known she was up there, and even now no one can really say. As for the old lady, she probably didn't mind how he had done it, only that he had managed to. For the rest of us it is just another example of how remarkable animals can be, and how they can sometimes do things which we simply never could.

KENLEY LASS: THE PIGEON WHO SPIED FOR BRITAIN

Supporting the Resistance, Second World War, France, 1940

Today it seems incredible that fixing a short message to a bird's leg can be a better way to communicate than using a radio or telephone. But the military regularly relied on pigeons during both world wars, as did many secret agents operating behind enemy lines.

By the Second World War most radio sets were still much too heavy to carry around and rarely very reliable. Their signals could also be detected by the enemy, and even without being decoded the sound of a message being sent could easily give away the agent's position and lead to them being captured or even killed.

Trained pigeons, such as Kenley Lass, were often the best alternative. Easy to transport, so they could be taken on operations, these birds could also find their way home very quickly when the agent needed to send a message back to headquarters. The system worked so well that in all several thousand pigeons were employed in the 1940s, assisting agents in France, Belgium and the Netherlands after these countries were invaded by Germany.

> Several thousand pigeons were employed in the 1940s

Sometimes the birds travelled in little wicker baskets containing supplies of birdseed and water. These would be dropped by parachute at a place where the agent would be waiting to collect them. At other times the birds travelled with the agent, sometimes stuffed inside socks which would be hidden away in armpits or jacket pockets. As such they provided some company for the agents, men and women, who were sent deep into occupied territory to get information about the enemy and blow up military facilities. Theirs was a lonely and very dangerous job, and many of them didn't see a friendly face from one day to the next.

Kenley Lass came from Cheshire in the north of England, and in 1940 she was sent to France with an agent code-named 'Philippe'. In the dead of night the pair crossed the English Channel in a small single-engined aeroplane called a Lysander, a type specially designed so it could land almost anywhere. Typically this meant landing in a field in the middle of nowhere, the agent jumping out as the aircraft turned around so the pilot could take off again before anyone in the area realised what was going on.

Philippe was employed by the Special Operations Executive (SOE), a top-secret organisation based in London which specialised in sending agents deep into occupied territory. Their role was to make life as hard as possible for the enemy. Often this meant helping local resistance groups attack military bases and convoys, or destroy bridges and railways to make it hard for troops to move around. As well as helping plan this sort of sabotage, Philippe collected valuable information about the enemy's new weapons and any future battle plans.

It was incredibly dangerous work, and many of the agents were captured, imprisoned and tortured

It was incredibly dangerous work, and many of the agents were captured, imprisoned and tortured. It was also highly dangerous for the birds, and of the more than sixteen thousand pigeons which went on spying missions fewer than two thousand made it home. Most were shot down by enemy soldiers who were ordered to look out for them, or killed by falcons specially trained to hunt them.

Kenley Lass was one of the lucky ones. Fast enough to dodge bullets, and nimble enough to avoid being savaged by a bird of prey, in October 1940 she flew more than one hundred and fifty kilometres back to a pigeon loft in Surrey. In the metal canister attached to her leg was a coded message from Philippe, advising SOE that his mission had been successful. It also said where in France he was hiding so that the following night the Royal Air Force could send one of its Lysanders to pick him up.

Even now we do not know any details about Philippe's assignment in France because after more than seventy years his mission there is still classified as top secret. For this reason nothing could be said at the time about the role of Kenley Lass in bringing him home. In fact it was only when the war ended that her story was finally told, and in 1945 she received a Dickin Medal – the highest honour for an animal in war – for being the first bird ever to make it home from a mission behind enemy lines.

ANTIS: AN AIRMAN'S GUARDIAN ANGEL
Escaping Eastern Europe, Cold War, Czechoslovakia, 1948

A young Alsatian called Antis had some amazing adventures with his master, a Czech airman called Václav Robert Bozděch.

Bozděch, whose friends all called him Jan, had fled to France when his country was occupied by the Nazis in 1939. He found a puppy while he was there, apparently in the ruins of a burned-out farmhouse. When France was in turn invaded by Germany in 1940 the two of them escaped to North Africa and then slowly made their way to England.

Keen to help liberate his country, Jan decided to join the Royal Air Force as a gunner. Together with many other exiled Czechs who had joined up, he was soon flying missions over mainland Europe. It was while flying back from one of these that he felt a light tap on his elbow. Assuming it was one of the crew trying to attract his attention, he turned round. To his astonishment it was Antis, who was panting heavily, and then suddenly collapsed onto the floor of the aircraft.

Jan had no idea what his dog was doing there, or how on earth he had clambered aboard the bomber without anybody noticing. He could see Antis was in trouble, however. His chest was heaving and Jan realised he was having difficulty breathing as the plane was flying so high. As quickly as he could he unclipped his own oxygen mask and put it over the dog's face, and after a few moments Antis showed signs of recovering.

Bombing raids were hard enough without having to share your mask, and of course having passengers of any sort on board was against regulations. Jan was sure he didn't want to repeat the experience, but Antis was equally sure that he wasn't going to be separated from his master. This meant refusing to be left behind – so every time Jan and the crew prepared to board the plane Antis would somehow smuggle himself on board.

Every time Jan and the crew prepared to board the plane Antis would somehow smuggle himself on board

The other airmen thought it was all very funny. They loved having Antis around, and some of them looked upon him as a symbol of hope that one day they would return home. After his crew had survived one particularly dangerous mission Jan realised that, for many of the airmen,

Antis was looked upon as a kind of lucky charm. Some of them felt the dog had a special knack for detecting danger, and it was true that Antis often seemed to sense something long before anyone else was aware of an enemy fighter approaching.

Because of this Antis was allowed to tag along, but Jan and the crew did their best to make sure none of the senior officers found out about it. In all they made about thirty flights together, during which time Antis was twice injured by anti-aircraft fire. On one of these occasions he was hurt quite badly, but managed to remain quiet and calm until the aircraft had landed safely. This impressive show of courage and fortitude really inspired the men.

Perhaps because of this, when the secret of his regulation-busting flights eventually leaked out Antis was treated as a hero. The crew were forgiven for breaking the rules, and from then on Antis became a very special mascot for the RAF's No. 311 Czechoslovak Squadron. When the war ended in 1945 Jan naturally looked forward to taking Antis home to meet his family.

Unfortunately his delight at being able to do this at last was to be short-lived. Very soon after Jan returned home, Czechoslovakia was again thrown into chaos, and by 1948 the Communists had seized power. Overnight Jan and his friends, men who had risked their lives for freedom and for their country, were declared enemies of the state. Knowing that he was in danger of being hunted down by the secret police, Jan now had to flee for his life for the third time.

Jan now had to flee for his life for the third time

Last time escape had meant France and then England, but this time Jan and a companion decided to head for Germany. The journey was much too dangerous to risk taking his wife and baby son along, but Jan knew he wanted Antis by his side. This wasn't just sentimentality or the need for companionship. By now Jan really did feel that his friend brought him good luck, and was confident that Antis would be able to warn him in advance if he was ever in danger.

He wasn't wrong. After a long trek through thick forest in the dead of night the two men were nearing the border with Germany, where they hoped to sneak past the guards. Jan noticed, however, that the closer they got to the border the jumpier Antis became. He whispered to his companion that even though they couldn't hear anything they might not be alone in the forest.

Suddenly the two men were dazzled by searchlights, and both ran for cover just seconds before the ground around them was raked by machine-gun fire. It was obvious now that it would be impossible to cross the border as they had planned to do, but at least neither of them had been injured thanks to the early warning Antis had given them.

Neither of them had been injured thanks to the early warning Antis had given them

They decided on a more roundabout route, one which was much longer but – they hoped – safer. Navigating a path through the forest, Jan said later, Antis was their 'guiding light'. By the following morning the two men had reached the border without being spotted and crossed to safety.

Jan was never able to return to Czechoslovakia safely and, forced to abandon his wife and baby, he decided to move back to England and start a new life there. Antis, of course, went with him. He never went up in another aeroplane and the two companions remained inseparable until, after thirteen years together, the brave dog died peacefully one night. For Václav Robert Bozděch, Antis was irreplaceable. He loved dogs with a passion, but he never felt the need to have another one.

Bamse: the sailors' guardian
North Sea patrols, Second World War, Scotland, 1940–45

The name Bamse is Norwegian, and means 'teddy bear'. But Bamse was hardly a toy. Standing on his back legs, with his front paws resting on your shoulders, one of the most famous dogs of the Second World War would have been about two metres tall.

Bamse was a St Bernard, a hardy mountain breed well suited to life in the Alps. Traditionally these huge dogs were used for rescuing travellers lost in the deep snow, but this one was a sea-dog, a sea captain's pet who spent much of his time living on board a Norwegian ship called the *Thorodd*.

During the Second World War the *Thorodd* spent long months patrolling the icy waters between Norway and Scotland as part of the Norwegian resistance. In 1940 Norway had been invaded by Germany, but the crew of the *Thorodd* had managed to escape to Scotland. With their captain, Erling Hafto, Bamse's owner, they were determined to free their country. Photographs taken at the time show Bamse wearing a Royal Norwegian Navy steel helmet, because officially he was part of this crew. It is hard to imagine what his duties might have been, however, because poor old Bamse didn't like the water and was often seasick.

He was a very special dog, though, with a great sense of fun. Before the war he had enjoyed being ridden around like a pony by Erling Hafto's four young children. But when their country was invaded Bamse was taken on board the ship, probably to keep Captain Hafto company and to remind him of the family he had been forced to leave behind.

He was a very special dog with a great sense of fun

Luckily, for such a large dog, Bamse was easy to feed because he would eat pretty much anything that was cooked up in the ship's tiny, cramped galley. He was also great company for the men during their long patrols at sea, and in quiet periods when he wasn't feeling sick he would sometimes join them for a game of football on deck (playing in goal, by the way). Bamse also spent a lot of time bounding up and down the deck, and only once slipped on the wet planking and fell overboard. When that happened half the sailors jumped into the bitterly cold water to save him, suggesting he was a very popular member of the crew.

With Norway under enemy control the *Thorodd* had been converted into a minesweeper on one of its trips to Scotland. The crews of minesweepers look for enemy mines, a kind of deadly floating bomb. The work is hard and very dangerous, the purpose being to destroy the mines before they can sink or damage other ships. The *Thorodd* was also fitted with a large anti-aircraft gun, a weapon which made a terrible noise, although Bamse quickly got used to it.

He became an important symbol of the fight for Norwegian freedom and independence

The ship frequently docked in one of several Scottish harbours to refuel, and on these occasions Bamse often followed the men off the ship. The people in the towns soon got to know him well, and to them he became an important symbol of the fight for Norwegian freedom and independence. He would also stand guard when no one was on board the *Thorodd*, but when he went into town he was welcomed at many of the pubs and cafés in which the off-duty sailors liked to relax.

On at least two occasions he saved a sailor's life. The first time was in the harbour area of Dundee when one of the *Thorodd*'s officers was threatened by a man armed with a knife. Bamse saw what was happening and charged at the assailant at full speed. With such a big animal it was a force no one could have resisted, and after being hit hard by Bamse's ninety-kilogram bulk the man was knocked straight into the water before he could do anyone any harm. He was quickly pulled out and arrested.

The second time Bamse saved a life was when he saw another sailor fall into the sea. Sensing that the man was drowning, Bamse barked and barked to alert the rest of the crew to what had happened. Maybe no one heard him, or perhaps they thought he was just fooling around. For whatever reason no one came running, so, overcoming his dislike of water, Bamse leapt in after the sailor. He didn't know it but the man couldn't swim, so it was very lucky that Bamse had such a long thick coat that the man was able to grab hold of it so that the dog could slowly tow him to safety.

Today in Scotland they still remember Bamse with great affection, as a friendly dog and a brave one. A few years ago Prince Andrew unveiled a lovely life-size statue of him gazing out to sea. Another just like it has been put up in Norway too. It has been carefully positioned to look back this way, so that all these years after he first went to sea, Bamse can still be seen keeping an eye out for sailors in trouble.

Sergeant Reckless: the mare who helped Marines

Battle of Panmunjom-Vegas, Korean War, Korea, 1952

Bought by an American soldier with his own money, Reckless was a young Mongolian racehorse who worked tirelessly carrying men and ammunition during one of the fiercest battles of the Korean War.

Chestnut coloured, with a white flash on her forehead and three white legs, Reckless was originally called *Ah Chim Hai*, which is Korean for

'Morning Flame'. This was a beautiful name for a truly beautiful animal, but after paying two hundred and fifty dollars, Lieutenant Eric Pedersen decided to call her Reckless after the nickname given to his own unit of the 5th Marine Regiment.

The men in Pedersen's Recoilless Rifle Platoon were known as the 'Reckless Rifles' because their work was so dangerous. Their recoilless rifles were powerful enough to destroy a tank, but the explosive backblast was easy to spot from a distance. This meant the enemy could quickly return fire and kill anyone manning such a weapon.

The ammunition for the guns was also heavy and awkward to carry, which is why Lieutenant Pedersen wanted a packhorse to help carry the load. His men could lift only two or three of the ten-kilogram shells at a time, but Pedersen reckoned a fit horse could carry three times that amount, even a relatively small one like Reckless.

A fit horse could carry three times more shells than the soldiers

It took a while to get her used to military life but during her first few weeks in camp Reckless became known as something of a character. Unusually, she was allowed to wander around the camp rather than being confined to a paddock and so got to spend a lot of time with the men.

Reckless loved to eat with the soldiers, and though not a big horse she quickly acquired a reputation for helping herself to everything she liked the look of. In particular she preferred scrambled eggs, peanut butter and bacon to grass or hay, and would often share the soldiers' rations whether they wanted to or not. She also developed a taste for beer and fizzy drinks, but on the advice of an army medic was limited to just one or two bottles a day.

When she wasn't eating or drinking Pedersen and his comrades trained

her as best they could, and they had a special pack-saddle sent over from America. Reckless was taught how to walk slowly and carefully through rolls of razor-sharp barbed wire, and to find shelter whenever she heard soldiers shouting 'incoming' – meaning that enemy shells were about to land.

Reckless leapt into the air when the first gun went off

Even with the training, her first time in battle was a terrifying ordeal, however, and several retired Marines later recalled how Reckless leapt into the air when the first gun went off. Although she was carrying a heavy load of half a dozen shells, all four of her hooves left the ground, and when she landed she was shaking uncontrollably. Fortunately she was unhurt, and a soldier called Monroe Coleman was soon able to calm her down. When another big gun fired she just snorted loudly, and by the third or fourth time she seemed to understand what was going on and knew to remain calm.

The problem of the explosive backblast meant that soldiers using the guns had to keep moving from one firing position to another. This was the only way to avoid being spotted and shot at, but it had to be done quickly and quietly. Reckless therefore had to take a different route across the battlefield each time ammunition needed to be delivered to soldiers manning the guns.

Luckily she was clever and a very quick learner, and during the Battle of Panmunjom-Vegas the marines were astonished to discover that she could do it on her own. Once she had been shown a route Reckless would simply trot off alone. Then, after being loaded up with more shells, she would find her way to wherever the gun had moved to. This left the soldiers free to concentrate on fighting, and reduced the chances of any of them being hit or wounded while escorting Reckless.

Of course Reckless could not avoid the gunfire, and she was hit and wounded twice during the battle. Fragments from an enemy shell cut her above one eye, another caught her on her left side. She kept working, though, and during the course of a single day of very fierce fighting, she carried nearly four hundred of the heavy shells over a distance of sixty kilometres. (To give some idea of what this means, the total weight of the shells was equivalent to three modern family cars.)

She carried nearly four hundred of the heavy shells over a distance of sixty kilometres

The battle raged on for several days, and today it is remembered as one of the most savage ever fought by the US Marines. At the end of it Reckless was promoted to 'Corporal Reckless' in recognition of her outstanding contribution, and then later to staff sergeant. She was also awarded two Purple Hearts, a very special medal awarded in the name of the president of the United States to soldiers killed or wounded on the battlefield.

No horse has ever received such recognition, but then Reckless was no ordinary horse. After the battle it emerged that she had carried several wounded men to safety as well as ammunition, and, more than sixty years on, Marines still describe how she helped win the day. She did this not just by carrying all those shells but also by setting an example to the men. As one of them said decades after the battle, 'It's difficult to describe the elation and the boost in morale that little white-faced mare gave the Marines as she outfoxed the enemy by bringing vitally needed ammunition up the mountain.'

In old age she enjoyed a happy retirement back in the USA, and in 2013 a life-size statue of her was erected outside the National Museum of the Marine Corps.

RIFLEMAN KHAN: A SAVIOUR FROM THE WAVES

The Battle of the Scheldt, Second World War, Dutch coast, 1944

Khan, a large and handsome Alsatian, was volunteered for war service after his young owner, eight-year-old Barry Railton, heard a radio programme. It said that the War Dogs' Training School was looking for dogs which were strong, fit and intelligent. They were to be trained for guard and patrol duty with the army and for rescue work. Others might work as messengers and mine detectors.

Barry loved his dog, but he thought if the country needed Khan then Khan ought to go. It was a big decision for any boy to make, but his parents agreed and, after training, Khan found himself serving with soldiers of the 6th Battalion of the Cameronians.

Also known as the Scottish Rifles, Khan's new unit was based in Scotland, but he was soon posted overseas with his handler, Corporal Jimmy Muldoon. The two of them worked well together and quickly formed a close friendship. In 1944 they were attached to an assault party ordered to recapture the Dutch island of Walcheren, which had been occupied by the enemy.

> He thought if the country needed Khan then Khan ought to go

To reach Walcheren they had to travel by boat and then wade ashore along a two-kilometre-long mud bank. The mud was very thick and sticky, and the men of the 6th Battalion were warned to expect shellfire from heavily armed defenders who were well dug in on the island.

From the start the fighting was intense, and advance parties of Canadian soldiers were twice beaten back by the sheer volume of explosive shells raining down on them from concealed guns. Dozens of men were injured in these attacks, and before the assault party could launch another attempt a group of Royal Marine commandos were sent ashore under cover of darkness to silence the big guns.

They managed to prevent some of the guns from firing again, but as Corporal Muldoon and his comrades began to make their way towards the shore more guns opened fire from further down the island. Seconds later the small assault craft in which Jimmy was travelling was coming under sustained fire. Before long one of the shells found its mark and hit the boat amidships, the blast pitching men, equipment and poor old Khan into the black icy stew of the North Sea.

Unable to see where they were, the men struggled to keep afloat. Weighed down as they were by their guns and equipment, the thick, freezing mud beneath their feet seemed to pull them further below the surface. Eventually a few of the stronger ones managed to make it ashore, including Khan, but then through the darkness Muldoon's voice could be heard calling his dog's name again and again.

> Unable to see where they were the men struggled to keep afloat

Muldoon, who was not a good swimmer, must have become stuck somewhere in the freezing ooze. The men had to take shelter from the gunfire raking the mud bank and shells which were whistling overhead. But knowing his master was in trouble, possibly hundreds of metres offshore, Khan unhesitatingly ran back into the water and began to swim against the tide of soldiers working their way towards land.

After a few minutes Khan had reached Muldoon, and taking the collar of the soldier's tunic between his teeth he managed somehow to drag him back to the shore. Exhausted and injured, Muldoon was clearly not up to fighting and, almost as if he recognised this, the dog pulled him across the mud bank and onto safer, more solid ground. Refusing to leave his master's side until he was rescued, Khan went with Muldoon when he was taken to an army field hospital for treatment.

The lucky soldier went on to make a full recovery, and Khan seemed none the worse for the experience. His gallantry had been witnessed by a number of other soldiers on the island, and when the pair returned to their regiment it was suggested that the dog's selfless behaviour be recognised officially. He was promoted on the spot to 'Rifleman Khan', and a few months later back in England Barry Railton was presented with a medal in Khan's name.

By this time, Jimmy was closer than ever to Khan, although he accepted that when the war finally ended the dog would probably have to go back to his family. He was sad about this, but understood why, and so must have been delighted when a year or so later he received a letter from Barry.

The letter said that along with several other canine heroes Khan had been invited to London for the National Dog Tournament. Barry wondered if Corporal Muldoon wanted to come along too, and of course Jimmy leapt at the opportunity and made arrangements to travel down from Scotland.

When Khan entered the tournament arena a few weeks later and saw his old comrade he was beside himself with excitement. He was a big dog and nearly knocked Jimmy down as he jumped up at him again and again. Most of those watching won't have known the full story of what had happened in Walcheren, but to everyone cheering from the stands it must have been impossible to ignore the warm friendship which still existed between man and dog despite their time apart.

Barry certainly couldn't ignore it, even though he still thought of Khan as his dog rather than anyone else's. He didn't want to give him up as he still loved him very much, but after a short conversation with his family he knew, once again, what he had to do. Rifleman Khan was handed over to Jimmy Muldoon, the man whose life he had saved, and the two best friends went home to Scotland together.

SERGEANT STUBBY: THE DOG WHO CAUGHT A SPY

Third Battle of the Aisne, First World War, France, 1918

Plug-ugly, but clever and courageous, Stubby was a tough-looking stray who made friends with an American platoon bound for Europe. Together they spent more than a year fighting in France, by the end of which Stubby had become one of the most famous animals in the whole of the war.

Stubby's time with the army began when he turned up one day at a training camp north of New York. No one knew where the mongrel had come from, and most of the soldiers tried to ignore him when he started begging them for food. Luckily for Stubby, one of the other soldiers, Corporal Robert Conroy, was a dog lover. He liked the look of this ugly mutt so he started feeding him scraps of meat and found him a bowl to stop him drinking from the camp toilets.

He liked the look of this ugly mutt so started feeding him

Before long the two of them were best friends, and when Conroy was off duty he was always seen playing around the camp with his dog. He came up with the name Stubby because the dog had such a short tail, and when Conroy heard his platoon was being posted to France, he decided to break the rules and take his new pal with him.

Stubby was part-bulldog and so not very big. Because of this Corporal Conroy thought he could probably hide him somewhere on board the ship taking the 102nd Infantry across the Atlantic. He managed it, too, only for the dog to be discovered as soon as the SS *Minnesota* docked in Europe and everyone disembarked.

During the voyage Conroy had taught the dog to lift his front paw like a salute, which he now did every time a senior officer went by. This had been done as a bit of a joke and to pass the time, but luckily the joke appealed to Conroy's commanding officer. He agreed the corporal could keep the dog as long as it was well-behaved, and so, despite a ban on soldiers keeping pets, Stubby was allowed to march off with the rest of the men to the trenches of the Western Front where the Americans were to defend France and Belgium against the Germans.

Once the fighting began no one ignored Stubby because even the soldiers

who didn't much like dogs found they enjoyed having one around during times of stress and danger. Stubby was a reminder of happier times for many of the soldiers, especially those who missed their homes and families. Because of this he was made a great fuss of whenever the men could find a moment to relax.

But Stubby was useful too, his outstanding sense of smell and sharp hearing proving invaluable to the other members of his platoon. It was Stubby, for example, who warned the men to take cover during artillery barrages. (He could hear the terrifying whine of an incoming shell seconds before the men could.) He was also in one of the trenches when the soldiers came under attack from special shells containing poisonous mustard gas. This was potentially deadly, but Stubby learned to recognise the smell and would bark excitedly whenever he detected it. When he did this the men would know to put on their gas masks and his, and he saved several lives in this way.

Altogether Stubby accompanied the men on four major offensives and took part in seventeen different battles when he would run up and down the trenches howling. At one time the platoon came under almost continuous fire for nearly a month, and Stubby was badly injured when a grenade exploded right by him. He had to have his leg stitched, but this was his only serious injury. When he could walk again he returned to his unit almost immediately, and began running around no man's land looking for wounded soldiers who needed help.

The dog's most astonishing adventure came very near the end of the war, however. During lulls in the fighting Stubby liked to patrol his territory, marching along the trenches making sure everyone was safe and accounted for. One day while doing this he came across someone he didn't recognise.

The man spoke to him in English, but Stubby was suspicious and started barking and howling loudly to alert the rest of the platoon. The man tried to silence the dog and calm him down, and when that failed he turned and ran for it. Stubby tore after him and, launching himself over one of the trenches, managed to pull him to the ground.

The two of them started rolling over and over, and the man put up a tremendous fight. Fortunately Stubby managed to lock his strong jaws painfully around the intruder's ankle and refused to let go. The man probably realised at that point that he wasn't going to escape and that he might as well stop struggling.

Within a few minutes help arrived in the form of several of Stubby's comrades, and the man surrendered and was led away to be interrogated. He turned out to be a German spy who had crawled through the woods to reach the Americans' position. A search found that he was carrying a detailed hand-drawn map showing the layout of the American trenches, something which would have been of immense use to the enemy during its next big attack.

Stubby was immediately declared the hero of the day and made an honorary sergeant for his vigilance and fortitude. As the first dog ever to be promoted in the American army, he was **Stubby was the first dog ever to be promoted in the American army** also awarded the French 1914–18 Commemorative War Medal, the American Purple Heart, and a special gold medal for service to his country. Despite all this the official ban on soldiers' pets meant that he still had to be secretly smuggled onto another ship in order to get home. Once there he received the welcome which he was due and, hailed as a hero and a celebrity, he was led into the White House by none other than the president of the United States of America.

MARY OF EXETER:
THE BIRD WHO WASN'T BEATEN
The French Resistance,
Second World War, France, 1942

Nicknamed the pigeon who wouldn't give up, Mary was volunteered for war service in 1940 and spent five years carrying secret messages back to England from agents in France.

Mary belonged to Charlie Brewer, a shoemaker from Devon who had raised her from an egg. Each time she completed a mission she would return to his pigeon loft in the historic West Country city of Exeter. It was Charlie's job to remove the message from a canister attached to her leg and make sure it reached the authorities.

Exeter was one of several beautiful English cities which were targeted by German bombers in an attempt to damage morale. It was hit repeatedly during the Blitz, and in one of these raids a huge bomb exploded just down the street from Charlie's house. The blast killed many of his best birds, but Mary escaped more or less unhurt. Charlie decided to move her to a safer building a few hundred metres away in case it happened again.

The blast killed many of his best birds, but Mary escaped

Two nights later the bombers were indeed back, and this time one of them targeted the very building Charlie had moved his birds to. This second explosion, even more ferocious than the first, caused a panic among the pigeons. This time Mary's cage was completely destroyed, but once again she was among the survivors.

More than two hundred and fifty people were killed in these raids, and much of the city was wrecked. To Charlie, though, it must have looked as though Mary was one of his luckier birds. She would have been terrified by the noise of the explosions and by the fires caused by the bombs, and twice she had come close to losing her life, but somehow she always seemed to survive.

It was much the same when Mary went on her missions. The messages she carried were always top secret, and even after the war had ended Charlie always refused to talk about them. All he would say was how brave his birds had been, and none more so than Mary of Exeter, his little bird who refused to give up.

On one occasion she disappeared for nearly a week after being parachuted with an agent into enemy-occupied France. The mission was top secret, and when Mary didn't return Charlie assumed she was lost for good. She might have been captured with the agent or killed by one of the hawks which were trained to catch pigeons carrying secret messages. His relief must have been enormous when Mary suddenly reappeared back at the loft a few days later, especially as the canister containing the vital message was still attached to her leg.

She'd lost about a third of her body weight and was clearly exhausted

Charlie could see she was in pretty poor shape, however, as she'd lost about a third of her body weight and was clearly exhausted. She was also bleeding badly from her neck. This suggested she had been attacked by a hawk, but Charlie knew it was incredibly rare for a pigeon to make it home after such an ordeal.

It took him a few weeks to nurse her back to health, and then she was off again. This next mission called for her to be dropped back in France with another agent. She flew home more quickly this time, much to Charlie's relief, only this time she had a section of one wing missing. Later he found three shotgun pellets embedded in her body.

Remarkably, she recovered from this too, and soon took off for a third mission to France with her shortened wing. This time she did not return, and Charlie reluctantly concluded that her luck had run out and that she was gone for good. It was very sad, but there was nothing he could do about it. Then, to his astonishment, someone he knew told him they had found a pigeon in a field outside the city. It seemed too much to hope for, but when Charlie went to find the bird he recognised her at once as Mary of Exeter.

The person who found her had described Mary as 'more dead than alive' and it was obvious that she was much too exhausted to fly the last few minutes back to the loft. Charlie picked her up and carried her back, and once again he noticed the tell-tale signs that she had been attacked by another hawk or falcon.

This one had left a long wound running from the top of her head down one side of her neck, and on her body she had several small but deep puncture marks from its claws. Mary was also having difficulty holding her head up but, cradling her in his arms, Charlie saw she still had the message, meaning that her mission had been a success.

Charlie hoped he could patch her up again, but knew that this might be the end for Mary – or at least the end of her flying career. Treating her **Treating her wounds required twenty-two stitches** wounds required twenty-two stitches, which someone later told Charlie was the equivalent for such a tiny bird of a grown man receiving four thousand! Determined to do what he could for her, Charlie made a special leather collar to support her head while she got some strength back into her neck muscles.

For the next couple of weeks it was touch and go, and once again Charlie faced the very real possibility that he might lose his most extraordinary bird. Every day he fed and watered her by hand and made a fuss of her, and bit by bit she began to recover. After another couple of weeks she began to show definite signs of improvement, and to Charlie's delight she eventually made a full recovery.

Having proved that she really wouldn't give up, Mary of Exeter remained 'on duty' with the National Pigeon Service for the rest of the war. We still don't know much about her missions, except that they were top secret and she completed them all. When she died she was buried alongside Rip and Tipperary Beauty, two of the hero dogs whose stories are in this book.

BOB: THE HERO DOG THEY HAD TO CAMOUFLAGE

Operation Torch, Second World War, French North Africa, 1942

A characterful Labrador–collie cross with strong black and white markings, Bob was an official army dog rather than a stray adopted by soldiers. A good companion as well as a highly skilled tracker when it came to sniffing out the enemy, in 1942 he was sent to North Africa with the Queen's Own Royal West Kent Regiment.

Bob took part in 'Operation Torch', a massive Anglo-American attempt to capture a large area of north-west Africa and mount new attacks on the Germans. This went well to begin with, but after a few weeks of

After a few weeks of fighting the two sides were stuck in a stalemate

fighting the two sides were stuck in a stalemate so neither side could make any real advances. Instead soldiers on both sides hunkered down in hidden positions, only taking occasional shots at each other.

Situated on slightly higher ground, the enemy were in a stronger position than the British troops and the men in Bob's unit had to take cover behind a low hill to avoid being shot. Any movement from them was met by deadly bursts of shell, mortar and gunfire, and it soon became clear that the only safe way for them to move around was under cover of darkness.

This meant that any patrols into enemy territory had to be carried out at night-time, requiring the men to blacken their faces so that they wouldn't show up in the moonlight. Because Bob was going with them he had to be camouflaged as well, and so all his white patches were carefully painted black.

While the stand-off between the two sides continued, these raids on the enemy were carried out nearly every night. Bob's main job was to run messages from one group of soldiers to another, something he was very good at. Extremely fast and able to cover great distances without making a sound, he carried the messages in a leather pouch strapped to his back.

On many of these raids Bob was accompanied by a company quarter-master sergeant called Robert Cleggett. The two were great pals and CQMS Cleggett soon learned that if Bob ever froze and refused to walk forward it was the clever dog's way of warning him that enemy soldiers were nearby.

One night Bob was out on patrol with a small group of soldiers trying to identify enemy positions. It was cold and very dark, and, as usual, his white bits had been carefully painted out to avoid him being spotted. Bob suddenly stopped, his signal that enemy soldiers were somewhere nearby. As the patrol leader couldn't see or hear anything he made the signal for the men to move on after a few moments' delay.

The men had been about to walk straight into an ambush

Bob still refused to move, however, and instead stayed rooted to the spot. One of the other soldiers said that perhaps the dog knew more than the patrol leader did, and that the enemy might be much nearer than they had thought. Luckily the leader decided to trust Bob on this occasion, and the men froze just like Bob had done. Seconds later a tiny sound was heard only a few metres away, showing that Bob was right and that the men had been about to walk straight into an ambush.

CQMS Cleggett said later that it was only Bob's warning that saved the patrol from an attack which would almost certainly have been fatal. But actually having him on the patrol was important in another way too. Knowing where the enemy was hiding meant the soldiers could return with reinforcements, and by helping them deal with the threat in this way Bob helped break the stalemate.

After this no patrol leader risked ignoring Bob's warnings again. The soldiers were brave men and they were very skilled at what they were doing.

But dogs have a keener sense of smell and much better hearing, and it was these which enabled Bob to alert the patrol to the danger they were in.

On several occasions after this Bob's incredible ability to sense trouble is known to have saved more soldiers' lives, but sadly he disappeared at the end of the war and was never seen again. The soldiers of the West Kents have never forgotten him, however, and today a life-size model of their hero dog is displayed at the regimental museum in Maidstone. This sits alongside Robert Cleggett's war medals, including a very special one presented to him in memory of his clever camouflaged dog.

GANDER: CANADA'S FEARLESS FRIEND

The Battle of Lye Mun, Second World War, Hong Kong, 1941

Some dogs chase cars, but Pal liked running after aeroplanes. A huge black Newfoundland who looked almost the size of a grizzly bear, his antics amused pilots and passengers at the airfield near where he lived in Canada. But it is not hard to imagine how dangerous it could be, having a dog on the runway, and eventually Pal's owner decided he would have to be sent away.

As he was such a big strong animal he was offered to the army, and they were delighted to have such a strong and magnificent-looking new recruit. Joining a regiment called the Royal Rifles of Canada, Pal soon found himself eating, sleeping and even showering with a friendly bunch of soldiers. They renamed him Gander, after the name of their base. In October 1941 the Rifles were shipped out to Hong Kong island, a British colony, to defend it against the Japanese, and Gander travelled with them as their lucky mascot.

Hong Kong soon came under heavy attack from both aircraft and ground troops, and the Canadians joined forces with British and Indian regiments, as well as many hundreds of local volunteers. Unfortunately, even with a combined strength of two thousand, the Canadians were still massively outnumbered.

In every way the situation looked bad. There were at least four attackers for every one defender, and with the nearest Royal Air Force base more than one thousand kilometres away the Canadians knew not to expect any help from that direction. Four or five old biplanes were available to take off from Hong Kong, but these were quickly destroyed by more than a dozen bombers.

There were at least four attackers for every one defender

Together with the British and Indian troops, the Canadians fought on bravely, ignoring appeals from the enemy to surrender and doing what they could against seemingly impossible odds. Defending an important coastal position called Lye Mun, Gander and dozens of the men were forced to retreat to a fortified bunker to escape a barrage of shells and incoming fire. This continued for a full week, wounding many of the men and leaving

Gander so scared that he struggled to leave the bunker when small groups of soldiers went out on patrol.

The intensity of the shelling could mean only one thing. Preparing to launch their final, decisive attack on Hong Kong, the enemy was trying to clear them out. When the attack began it was terrifying. Canadian observers estimated that three full regiments were zeroing in on Lye Mun: literally thousands of heavily armed men determined to wipe out the last of the defenders.

Gander suddenly sprang into action, almost as if he realised that this was his moment to star. As enemy soldiers began to pour onto the beach at Lye Mun, Gander forgot his fear and seemed to be in his element. Unfazed by the explosions, and ignoring all the bullets whistling over his head, he began barking and biting, snarling and rising up on his hind legs like the huge bear he so resembled.

They all turned and ran as soon as they saw him bounding out of the undergrowth

Most of the enemy troops had probably never seen such an enormous dog, and some of them might even have mistaken Gander for an actual bear. This would certainly explain why they all turned and ran as soon as they saw him bounding out of the undergrowth towards them. It could also be the reason why, when he started snapping at their heels, not one of them thought to just pull out a gun and shoot the dog dead.

Gander didn't care what the reason was. He carried on attacking the enemy again and again, rushing at them from concealed positions, and doing everything he could to harry them and drive them back. This gave the men behind him the opportunity they needed to reload their weapons and prepare to fight back, and after a few of Gander's charges it became apparent that the enemy had had enough.

None of the Canadians was foolish enough to think this meant they had won the battle, particularly when so many of them were injured and could not leave the bunker. In fact all it meant was that the attackers were too scared to come face to face with the black beast again, and that they would be trying to think of a different way to continue their assault.

For a minute or two everything went quiet, and then grenades started exploding around the men. The Canadians realised the danger immediately and were able to toss several of the grenades back at the enemy before they exploded. A couple of these found their mark and detonated, and then one landed among a group of seven injured soldiers, none of whom was able to reach out and throw it back.

If you are faced with a grenade you have only a very few moments before it explodes, but on this occasion none of the able-bodied soldiers was near enough to reach it in time. Gander was right on the spot, however, and he realised at once what he needed to do. Like any dog with a ball, he gathered up the grenade in his jaws, and, in what could only be a fatal manoeuvre, he ran back down the hill towards the person who threw it.

He must have looked as terrifying as ever, and the enemy troops couldn't get away fast enough when they realised what he was holding in his mouth. The Canadians cheered him on loudly, but realised too that the dog's selfless and courageous action meant that he was doomed. In the end Gander was

The dog's selfless and courageous action meant that he was doomed

able to save the lives of all seven injured men, but sadly he lost his own when the grenade finally exploded.

Happily, the big dog who liked to chase aeroplanes has never been forgotten in Canada as his name was officially listed among the more than five hundred Allied officers and men who fought and died trying to save Hong Kong. His story might have ended there, but for the efforts of several survivors of the battle who were determined to see their dog's heroic self-sacrifice recognised for what it was.

One of the soldiers at Lye Mun had been given the Victoria Cross, the highest award for bravery, and the men of the Royal Rifles felt Gander deserved something similar. They felt this so strongly that they spent years writing letters to various government and military authorities with eye-witness accounts of Gander's brave deeds. It took a while, but eventually their efforts paid off. In 2000 – nearly sixty years after the events of Lye Mun – Gander was awarded the Dickin Medal, the animal Victoria Cross, for saving so many Canadian lives.

EPILOGUE
The Animals in War Memorial

For a country whose people are so fond of animals it took a surprisingly long time for Britain to recognise properly the heroism of literally millions of feathered and four-legged creatures.

A few of their stories have made the news over the years, and some animals have been rewarded with medals. But these are only a tiny fraction of those who have served alongside the armed forces and whose heroic actions are still recalled with warmth and affection by the soldiers, sailors and airmen and women who knew them. Their contribution has been incredible, with thousands of people owing their lives to animals like the ones described in this book.

London's Animals in War Memorial is intended finally to acknowledge the sacrifice these heroes have made on our behalf. It was unveiled in 2004 by Her Royal Highness The Princess Royal. No individual animals are named on the graceful stone and bronze memorial near Hyde Park, but only because there are too many to name. Instead the memorial includes carved representations of the different species which have come to the aid of our servicemen and women, and lists the places where battles have been fought and won.

On one side two life-size sculptures of exhausted, heavily laden mules are shown approaching a narrow gap in an otherwise impenetrable twenty-metre wall. On the other a horse and dog walk on. The dog is glancing back towards the wall, as if remembering his fallen comrades, but the pair are seen walking into a brighter, better future – a future free of war.

It's a very special place, and hopefully if you visit this part of London you will go and see it. Take a few minutes to think about the animals you have read about here, but remember they are only the tiny minority, the ones whose stories are known. Millions went with them, and every one deserves our thanks.

FOR AS LONG AS PEOPLE HAVE LOOKED FOR ADVENTURE,
SOME HAVE ALSO FOUND DANGER . . .

SURVIVORS

EXTRAORDINARY TALES FROM THE WILD AND BEYOND

DAVID LONG · KERRY HYNDMAN

WHEN IT COMES TO EXTREME STORIES OF SURVIVAL, FEW CAN MATCH THESE TRUE TALES OF HEROISM

Ranging from classics such as Shackleton's expedition to the Antarctic, to more modern exploits, including the adventurer who inspired the movie *127 Hours*, these courageous survivors all have one thing in common: an incredible ability to draw on all their strength, bravery and self-belief in order to beat the odds, and live to tell their tales . . .

Coming in Autumn 2019 . . .

RESCUE

Remarkable real-life rescue missions.

How far would you go to save a life?

Scrambling from the wreckage of his school
after an earthquake, a nine-year-old Sichuan
boy rescued two unconscious friends. 'I
was hall monitor,' he said afterwards. 'It is
my job to look after my classmates.'

Whether dragging a friend from a blazing car,
masterminding a search far below the earth's surface,
or recovering astronauts from an aborted space
mission, RESCUE reveals the ingenuity, courage and
doggedness of the human spirit all over the world.